PEG and I

Potato

PEG and I

Nancy Grafton

ISIS
LARGE PRINT
Oxford

First published in Great Britain 2001
by ELSP

Published in Large Print 2004 by ISIS Publishing Ltd,
7 Centremead, Osney Mead, Oxford OX2 0ES
by arrangement with the Author

British Library Cataloguing in Publication Data
Grafton, Nancy 1920–
    Peg and I: her story of a childhood on a Wiltshire
    farm. – Large print ed.
    – (Isis reminiscence series)
    1. Grafton, Nancy, 1920– – Childhood and youth
    2. Farm life – England – Wiltshire – History –
    20th century
    3. Large type books
    4. Wiltshire (England) – Social life and customs –
    20th century
    5. Wiltshire (England) – Biography
    I. Title
    942.3'1083'092

ISBN 0–7531–9940–8 (hb)
ISBN 0–7531–9941–6 (pb)

Printed and bound by Antony Rowe, Chippenham

To Peg
and in Memory of Dick and Barbara

CONTENTS

FOREWORD

It was on a visit to the old farm at Stockley that I first decided to write this book.

On a hot day in June — the first warm day of that particular year, I was sitting on the sheltered lawn in front of the rambling old house. The grass, so soon to lose its colour with the drought, was green and lush after the spring rain and Dick's hanging baskets of ivy leafed geraniums framed the porch, their pink and mauve blossoms lifted to the midday sun. The front door was open and the clatter of dishes from the kitchen gave me a happy sense of perpetuity.

But I fell to wondering, this beloved house that had stood for centuries, how long could it continue? Would not some architect in the distant future decide that the old walls leaned too far for safety or suggest extensive alterations far too costly to be practical? Would it then be replaced with some more modern edifice, with fitted carpets, fitted kitchen and fitted bathroom?

Perhaps in the next century Dick's descendants would look at faded colour photographs of Great Grandfather's flowers in the front of the house. The more imaginative of them might wonder what lay behind the casement windows but there would be nobody living to tell them. No-one who had raced up the crooked stairs, no-one who had sat round the log fire in the drawing room on a winter's night, when the wind whistled in the fir trees outside.

So I decided, before I left my deckchair that afternoon, that in the near future I would try to pen down some of the things, sad and happy, that happened so long ago.

Because I found it difficult, if not quite impossible, to separate the events of my own life from that of my twin, I entitled it *Peg and I*.

Nancy Grafton, Cherhill

PART ONE

CHAPTER ONE

The Family

My twin and I were born on a blustery spring day in March 1920 at Stockley Farm, Stockley, Calne, in Wiltshire. A multiple birth not being expected, Peg's arrival twenty minutes after my appearance in the world caused great consternation and amazement to the rest of the family, the family doctor and in fact the entire village. Only brother Dick and older sister Barbara were singularly unaffected by this unexpected happening. Having always, for the whole of their short lives, shared everything and been treated scrupulously "alike", they felt it was only fair that they should each have a baby sister.

Doctor Ferguson, who had arrived at the farm during the afternoon in his old coupé, sportingly offered to adopt one of us. Whether this was to make amends for not correctly anticipating the advent of twins, or whether he was genuinely interested in adoption, I shall never know. However, having got over the initial shock, Mother would not, of course, part with either of us. Which was just as well as I, being the first born and half a pound heavier, would probably have been the one to go!

Thus we started life at the farm, just when the world was supposed to be recovering from the Great War. Farming was a hazardous occupation in those years between the Wars and, in spite of long working hours, there was little to be made at it. All our relatives seemed more affluent than we were, perhaps they were better at business than Dad and Mother. The welfare of their animals meant more to our parents than making hard cash out of them. I wonder what either of them would make of today's factory farming methods?

Peg and I had a very happy childhood. Mother was fully trained as a teacher and she taught us at home until we were nine and a half years old (this book is about these pre-school years). We had such a lot of opportunities to explore the countryside, the village and to run wild on the farm. We were a complete unit Peg and I, requiring no other companions, we were quite happy on our own. Together we could face anything, or so it seemed in those far off days. Tiffs we might have, but let anyone dare to disagree with one of us, then the other would immediately fly to her defence.

Peg, in spite of being the youngest and the smallest, was also the more dominant one and I suppose I relied on her to make most of the decisions.

Dad, quiet and unassuming with a dry sense of humour, was devoted to his home and family. His parents, well-to-do strict members of the Plymouth Brethren Sect, had ruled their family rather firmly. His life at boarding school had been rather austere and exacting. In contrast we were allowed quite a lot of freedom and, I am sure, received more than our fair share of affection.

Mother was small, energetic and dynamic. Everything she did was done at speed — I don't think she ever walked slowly in her life and when cycling she was always in the lead, pedalling furiously up all the hills. I don't think it was quite the thing to pass Mother on a bike. Taking advantage of a level bit of road, Barbara did once overtake her. I suppose the enormity of this act must have struck her immediately and she tried to regain her right side of the road quickly. Too quickly, in fact, because she touched Mother's front wheel as she did so, causing her bike to career over the narrow grass verge coming to rest with spinning wheels on the edge of the road, whilst Mother shot over the hedge. It was no time for hilarity then, although we have all laughed about it since. Barbara says she can still see Mother's angry face as she parted the bushes and rose from the undergrowth.

Our lessons must have taken up quite a lot of her time, but she always seemed to be able to combine teaching with doing some of her housework. She started giving us lessons when we were about four years old, commencing with the art of pothooks and how to hold a pencil correctly. We gradually progressed from there until we were getting two hours of lessons in the morning and another session of an hour in the afternoon. We had no real holidays, apart from public holidays, so we didn't really have the chance to forget what we had learnt. We would sit at the kitchen table and write and do sums whilst Mother was making pastry. Every now and then she would leave her mixing bowl and stand behind us, pointing with a floury finger at a spelling mistake or an incorrect addition. Our tables we would chant aloud, our voices rising to a crescendo when Mother left the kitchen to wash up in the scullery; she would then be able to hear us and prompt or correct when we went wrong.

Mother had an intense love of animals and would befriend anything in the nature of a stray, whether it was dog, cat or a wild thing. Her love of flowers was reflected in the beauty of the borders at the farm. She was not fanatical about the housework but loved all the work connected with the countryside — the jam, pickle and wine making especially.

There was always something brewing in the large brown crock on the pantry floor, either dandelion wine or Mother's speciality — lemon beer. She had one unforgettable experience with the latter — bottled too soon, it exploded with a series of large reports, leaving the ceiling of the cupboard under the stairs stained. For a while the whole house smelt like a brewery.

Every week Mother made butter, some for our own use and some for sale to a grocers in Calne. We had a small butter churn with legs that would stand on the kitchen table. Mother would put the required amount of cream into the churn and one or the other of us would turn the handle that worked the wooden paddles. The cream would "slurp slurp" against the sides of the churn until the lump of butter formed and the whole rhythm changed as it now banged against the sides. The butter had "Come" was the expression we used. I generally read a book at the same time as doing my stint at churning and sometimes I would be so engrossed in my story that the butter would "Come" unnoticed. This apparently didn't do it any good as Mother liked to tip the pale yellow mound immediately onto the marble slab and pat it roughly into shape with the ridged wooden butter pats.

Crab-apple jelly was another of Mother's specialities. She made vast quantities of this and sold it along with the butter to Wiltshire, the grocers, in Calne. Blackberry jelly was made in the early autumn, to be enjoyed later with toast for winter afternoon teas. I remember the unfortunate day Mother had made a large pan of jelly. It stood on the shelf in the scullery, waiting for its final boiling with sugar. Barbara, clearing the tea things from the kitchen in a rush to finish, absent-mindedly poured a teapotful of cold tea leaves into the jelly. Aghast we tried to think what we could do about this tragedy, even considering pouring the whole lot back through the tea strainer. This hardly seemed feasible as, by now, the beautiful deep purple liquid was a dirty brown shade. In the end Barbara had to own up and face Mother's wrath and the offending liquid was thrown away. It is a wonder Mother didn't boil the mixture up and see if it was possible to make "Bramble Tea Jelly". It might have produced unknown medical properties.

Mother was rather interested in Nature's cures. In the spring we had dandelion sandwiches and later in the year must have eaten vast quantities of boiled stinging nettles, both supposed to be very good for the blood. I am quite sure our families must have been the purest in the County. Mother read that soot was good for the teeth so, once a month, we cleaned our teeth with that. I am not quite sure if it improved our teeth but it meant that we had a row of pale grey toothbrushes. Later we switched to bicarbonate of soda — this was easier on the toothbrushes but left a most unpleasant taste in the mouth. We had to have a sweet to take this taste away which rather defeated the object.

Mother must have been very modern for her generation, although I don't think we realised or appreciated it at that age. In fact when we went to Weston-Super-Mare for the day and she bathed in her black costume with the white rubber cap, we felt slightly embarrassed. The other mums might paddle, skirts held high on the edge of the sea but Mother and Auntie Dora were splashing and leaping around like a couple of playful porpoises several yards out in the muddy water.

I mention Auntie Dora here because she was so much a part of our childhood that it doesn't seem right to postpone writing about her until a later chapter. Mother's unmarried youngest sister, she was on call in times of illness or sorrow. She was at the farm when Peg and I was born and stayed on for months until Mother could cope with her much enlarged family. She would reappear when measles or some other epidemic laid us low. At the same time, she shared in our joys as well as our sorrows and Christmas was always that much more enjoyable when she could spend it with us. We all loved her dearly.

Dick was seven and Barbara was five when we were born. By the time we were old enough to appreciate their company, they had their own school friends and the age group meant quite different interests.

CHAPTER
TWO

The Farm

No one seems to know just when the farm was built. It is thought to be over 300 years old. At the very early part of the century, a wing was built on at the back. The rooms here are large and the ceilings high, but the old part of the house is long and sprawling and badly planned.

The bedrooms in particular seemed most inconvenient. They were fairly adequate when we were on our own, but all their shortcomings became apparent when we had someone to stay. For instance, the spare room was in the centre of the house. If you slept in either of the two bedrooms to the east of this one, you had to go down the front stairs, through the kitchen and up the back stairs to reach the bathroom and avoid barging through the guest's room.

There was one bedroom at the end of a long passage. Here Dick slept, the scientist and brains of the family. The large table in front of the window was crammed with bottles, jars, test tubes and queer coloured liquids that bubbled and smelt as they heated on spirit lamps. It shows what faith our parents had in their children. I don't think they ever envisaged the house being blown up around them. Peg and I were fascinated by this room and would creep in and gaze around. The whole place took on a sinister appearance, the wind sighed in the fir trees outside in the garden and their dark branches excluded part of the light.

There was a cupboard in this room and Dick and Barbara had discovered that, when the loose boards were prised away from the back, one could enter a passage that stretched along the inside of the corridor to the front stairs. Known as *"the secret passage"*, we wove a lot of imaginary tales about why it came to be there, although I suppose it was nothing more sinister than an error on the part of the builders. Dick's room also housed the airing cupboard with its noisy hot water tank. Here the near boiling water gave out half strangled gulps and gurgles before flowing through the yards of piping in the roof space to the bathroom at the other end of the house. After its long journey it would be little more than luke warm.

"The water's nearly cold!" Peg and I would chorus, as we sat each end of the large iron bath. Mother would then pound up the back stairs, a kettle of hot water in each hand and pour the contents into the middle of the bath. Peg at the tap end, which befitted her smaller stature, and I at the other end would sit with our knees under our chins, whilst the comforting warmth crept around us.

Mother once painted the bottom of the old iron bath. It looked beautiful, where there had been countless yellow stains all was now "whiter than white".

"Amazing what a difference a coat of paint makes," Mother said, tapping the hard gloss, "Arctic finish." whilst we all stood around admiringly.

All was well until the first hot bath. I think it was Barbara who discovered that the bottom of the bath was gradually getting soft and tacky, until she was forced to leap out onto the thick bath mat, her extremities covered with a thin layer of paint. This happened on every occasion: the hotter the bath, the more the paint melted. Finally it was necessary to buy another bath. The old one was demoted to the pig run where it was used as a drinking trough. I gathered that with cold water the paint stayed hard because the pigs thrived and there were no cases of lead poisoning.

The water for the bathroom had to be pumped from the deep well by a large hand pump in the milk house. When the big tank above the front stairs was empty it took 327 strokes of the pump to fill it. If it hasn't been noticed that the overflow pipe was running, the water would cascade down the front stairs, along the passage and out the back door.

Mother and Dad slept in the large bedroom in the new part of the house, which was reached by a small flight of stairs. The four of us moved in here once when we all developed measles — it was the only bedroom capable of holding all our beds. Here we sulked and quarrelled and fretted through a fortnight of the most beautiful spring weather until the spots went and we were able to go out into the sun.

The kitchen at the farm should, by rights, have been draughty and cold as four doors opened out of it — the one to the front hall, another to the scullery, the third to the back stairs and the last to the passage leading to the back door. Somehow it was quite a cosy room, with its old-fashioned range and the long low windowsill full of geraniums the whole year through. Green leafed and bright flowered in the summer, denuded of leaves and "leggy" in the winter.

On the other hand, the dining room, part of the new portion of the house, was a high, cold room. It faced north and the fire always seemed sulky and wouldn't blaze like it should. Large portraits of Grandfather and Grandmother Cole hung each side of the fireplace. We thought that Grandfather might have a ghost of a smile lurking behind his white beard so perhaps he had a sense of humour like Dad but Grandmother looked down from the large gilt frame disapprovingly. We had never known either of them so perhaps they were misjudged.

We like the drawing room. One of its windows looked out over the lawn, the other to the vegetable garden with the orchard in the distance. Here it was warm on winter nights, yet when the sun scorched the borders along the front of the house and waves of heat rose from the old red bricks, it was cool. The piano lived here and Mother would play *"Rustle of Spring"* and *"Over the Waves"* and Dad's favourite *"The Robin's Return"*. *+ " my sweet little people*

Opening from the brick shed at the back of the house was Dad's workshop and further on was the Back Kitchen which served as a playroom for all of us. Here on winter nights we would roast chestnuts and potatoes through the bars of the big fireplace, play table tennis and cards of the big deal table. The back kitchen had another attraction; it had a trap door in the ceiling leading to the Box Room. The Box Room had shelves all down one side to store the season's apples and the rest of the room was taken up with trunks of books, old Christmas cards etc., etc. Here Peg and I spent many a rainy afternoon, sitting on the floor with our backs against the high domed trunk. The little windows at the end looked out over the cowyard and we heard the clink of the churns on the cobbles and Dad, his head bent against the driving rain, could be seen going into the dairy.

On one side of the porch at the front door of the farm grew a white jasmine and on the other a honeysuckle and they intermingled at the top in a profusion of white and cream — the scent was intoxicating. The end of the house was clothed in virginia creeper which grew fiery red as the autumn days grew shorter. A *Gloire de Dijon* rose climbed up to the windows of our bedroom and Peg and I could lean out and see it clambering over the drainpipes. The "Old Glory" as we used to call it was the first to open its creamy apricot buds in the summer and the last to give way to autumn frosts.

A grapevine which bore sweet yellow grapes took up most of the other space on the wall of the house. Mother planted wallflowers, forget-me-nots and pink tulips in the long border in front of the house. They were quickly followed by the purple and white spire of canterbury bells and white arabis spilled over the stone trough in front of the back kitchen door.

Tall fir trees separated the lawn from the vegetable garden and very little would grow in the soil underneath them. The only plant that could compete with their roots was the hard honesty and here it flourished in a carpet of carmine and white, followed by the silvery seed heads which in turn provided the flowers for the following year.

Between the tall lilacs by the road and house was the lawn and here we played croquet.

Croquet was very much part of our childhood summers. I suppose in those more leisured days and before the advent of television and the mass exodus to the sea, it was played on long summer evenings and drowsy Sunday afternoons.

Our lawn would not by any stretch of imagination have been the best in the district but it was by far the most interesting. At one time I think there must have been a pond in the front of the house, long since filled in, but in the corner by the final hoop and peg there was a decided hollow, reminiscent of the shallow bunker of a golf course. This we christened "*The Dead Sea*". To add to our handicaps there was also "*The River Jordan*". This took the form of the long stone path leading from the front door to the front gate, neatly cutting off two hoops and a peg from the rest of the lawn. Crossing "*Jordan*" was a hazardous affair and guaranteed to send the most accurately positioned balls "off course". With many games of practice the family became quite expert at overcoming these obstacles and

15

would be several hoops ahead, whilst tearful cousins and tight lipped aunts and uncles wasted shot after shot trying to master *"The Dead Sea"* and *"The River Jordan"*. No doubt they got their revenge when return matches were played on their large, level lawns and the results of the games depended entirely on the player's skill.

At the end of the lawn there were a few shrubs and flowers and one dark red moss rose. In recent years I have tried several times to purchase a real old fashioned moss rose, but have never yet found one to equal the colour and perfume of the one at the end of the croquet lawn at Stockley Farm. I think if I ever do I shall be transported in my mind back to my childhood and be once again retrieving a croquet ball that had boundaried by that moss rose.

In front of the dining room window was another little sheltered lawn and by the side of this Mother grew her roses. She had a lovely collection of old-fashioned varieties, including the old Jacobite rose, *Maiden's Blush*. There were cabbage and moss roses, the old striped *York and Lancaster* and climbing over wooden arches were the rambling *American Pillar* and *Dorothy Perkins*.

The produce from the vegetable garden never really equalled Mother's flowers. The soil here was heavy with clay and there seldom seemed enough time to keep it free from weeds. We liked the fruit garden. The currant bushes would be festooned with old net curtains when the fruit was ripe, although I don't think this deterred the birds a great deal. There was one very old white currant bush that bore sweet currants which were delicious with cream and sugar.

Long after the main crop had been picked, we'd find a few overripe gooseberries, overlooked by Mother and the birds. One would sink one's teeth into them and the sweet liquid would pour down the throat like sampling a liqueur.

There was a garden frame in the corner by the orchard and Peg and I had one section of it for our own use. Here we planted lettuce seed far too thickly so that it never got beyond the seedling stage as we were loathe to thin it out. Our tomato plants generally got the blight from the neighbouring potatoes. One year, however, we did manage to grow a very large marrow which was our pride and joy for weeks.

Just through the wicket gate loading from the yard was a shrubbery of white ash, in the midst of which grew a cider apple tree — its twisted trunk and lichened branches stretching out of the thicket. Whatever sort of an apple season it was, this old tree bore a profusion of small green sour apples which made a marvellous jelly but was of little other use.

A path through the shrubbery led to the outside lavatory, seldom used then. It had a great fascination for Peg and me because it was a "three-seater" affair. Did former residents of Stockley Farm visit it "en masse", we wondered? Occasionally the lavatory had a good spring clean, whitewash was splashed on the plaster walls and the brick floor was scrubbed, but normally it was a cobwebby, dusty place, only to be used in extreme emergency. One could, of course, push the heavy wooden door shut and sit there and read for hours without being disturbed, which was a great advantage.

CHAPTER
THREE

Work and Play

Peg and I read a great deal and at quite an early age. We found *Black Beauty*, and in fact, any books about animals which were ill-treated, very sad and wept copiously. But the sufferings of the little heroine in *The Wide, Wide World* left us unmoved.

I loved dramatic poems and found Peg a willing and appreciative audience, although I doubt very much whether either of us could understand them. Peg would even burst into tears at my more dramatic passages, which was most gratifying.

> O Mary, go and call the cattle home,
> And call the cattle home,
> And call the cattle home
> Across the sands of Dee

was one of my favourites.

For a long time I enjoyed making up ghost stories which I related to Peg after we had gone to bed. They became more and more lurid until one night Peg walked in her sleep, falling halfway down the back stairs and I got the blame. After that Mother suggested that all my stories should have a happy ending which cramped my style no end.

Later some well meaning relative gave us a copy of *Grimms' Fairy Stories* and we got so wrapped up in Snow White and Rose Red and the Wicked Dwarf, to say nothing of the Frog Prince and Giant Golden Beard, that we both began to get nightmares. Mother took the book away and it was replaced with *What Katy Did* and *What Katy Did at School*. We really got hooked on these books and could hardly wait till Christmas to get *What Katy Did Next*.

On Sundays Mother would read "*Line Upon Line*" to us. Barbara shocked all of us once by saying "Oh, not those Christlike stories again, why can't we have something else!" We quite expected her to be struck dead at such blatant blasphemy but she survived and eventually married "into the cloth" so it was probably only a temporary lapse.

We didn't have a great number of toys, apart from Christmas and Birthday presents, which generally took the form of books or jigsaw puzzles or something else quite simple and inexpensive. We generally made do with home-made things. Dad, however, did once attend an auction sale at one of the large Country Houses in a neighbouring village and came back with two beautifully made purchases. This sale must have occurred when Peg and I were babies because one of the objects he brought was a twin pushchair.

Two beautifully carved horses were on the front and when the wheels revolved the two horses appeared to gallop, one rising high in the air, whilst the other plunged downward. Attached to the horses' heads were long reins which could be held by the occupants of the pushchair. According to members of the family who used to wheel Peg and me out for walks, our imposing chariot would frighten the life out of Topsy, a brown pony belonging to Auntie Edie. Our Auntie Edie lived at that time at Lower Farm, Heddington. When Topsy was seen approaching down the road, drawing the smart little pony trap, whoever was in charge of the pushchair had to drag it hurriedly onto the grass verge and stay there motionless until Topsy, shying and backing away, had been persuaded to pass by.

Dad's other wonderful buy was "The Boat" which was used on the lawn during the summer. The big wooden frame would hold quite a few children and grown-ups at each end. With a combined effort from all the passengers, it would start to rock until it gathered enough speed to carry on by itself.

Peg and I had the usual fads for toys that were in fashion at that particular time. We were given two wooden hoops, which gave us a lot of pleasure. Dad then produced two iron ones, probably off some defunct cart or other and these we found even better. He also made two hooped iron bars to guide them with, and they made a lovely harsh noise as we dashed up and down the road.

Skipping ropes were popular for a while and we found an old roller skate from somewhere or other and managed to travel around on that.

We had dolls, of course, but somehow I don't think we got a great deal of pleasure out of them, at least we didn't seem to play with them in the orthodox manner. They were either all ill in bed, in which case we pretended to dose them with different sorts of physic, or else they had multiple injuries from an accident and were bandaged up to their eyebrows. In our dilapidated doll's pram one of the cats was generally being pushed around, lovingly covered up with an old blanket and enjoying every moment of this unexpected attention.

We were not always happy, good-natured children. In fact, we could be quite the reverse.

"Peg and Nan are rather comical this morning." Mother would confide to Dad. A peculiar expression to describe our own particular brand of stubbornness and bad humour.

It only wanted one of us to feel disgruntled and the other immediately joined forces and, jointly, we were quite a formidable pair to be reckoned with.

Dick and Barbara were the proud possessors of two old-fashioned bikes, both with carriers and, on some occasions Peg would ride behind Barbara and I would be Dick's pillion passenger. Normally though we would be quite happy to see them go off on their own but sometimes we would decide that we should be allowed to go with them.

"You could take them just this once," cajoled Mother.

"Oh do we have to?" Dick would say.

"It will spoil everything," gloomily from Barbara.

Having made our impassioned plea, Peg and I stood by, wearing hurt, deprived looks.

In the end Dick and Barbara peddled sulkily down the road with their unwelcome burdens on the carriers. "Victory is ours", and "Justice seen to be done", we weren't really keen to be going at all.

"Sit tight or you'll fall off," cautioned Barbara.

"Keep your legs out or you'll get them in the wheel," instructed Dick as we swept over Weaver's Bridge.

By the tones of their voices we gathered they would not have been unduly upset if either of these eventualities happened. *Danny Kay*

When we reached the age of nine, it was felt that we ought to have bikes of our own so that we could really get proficient at riding them before we had to travel the three miles into Calne to school the following year. Mother was fortunate enough to get a child's bike from the owner of the local cycle shop but he didn't have anything suitable for me. With great initiative he made up a bike from a few odd parts he had lying around. The wheels could have come from a child's bike but the frame was large and long. Even with the saddle and handlebars at their lowest level, I still had to stretch my fat little arms and legs to reach the handlebars and the pedals.

However we were thrilled with these bikes and soon I had learnt to get on without help and Peg has mastered the art of dismounting without assistance. This worked quite well as I could get Peg started and then mount my awkward steed and catch her up. At the the end of the journey it was a case of Peg riding ahead for a few yards, jumping off and then coming to my help, hanging on to my handlebars whilst I slid to the ground from my high seat.

Having bikes meant that we could get much further afield; we could cycle to Heddington, push our bikes up the steepest part of Heddington Hollow and then ride across the rough track to Oliver's Camp and on over the downs until we were nearly at the Roundway and Devizes. We could also travel in the other direction; cycle up the Old Bear Lane past Bell Farm until the thatched cottages of Sandy Lane could be seen through the trees.

Avoiding main roads, it was surprising the number of miles we covered, Peg speeding up all the hills with her small gears but I making all the headway on the level.

Most of the summer seemed to be dominated by haymaking. It could stretch from June until September, depending on the weather and the crops. I suppose we were as mechanised as most of the farms in the area but the whole process from the cutting of the grass until it eventually reached the rick was a lengthy one.

Dad was up early those mornings to mow the dewy grass. He used a two-horse mower and by breakfast time the field would probably be half-cut. The moon daisies in the thick rows of grass already wilting as the sun climbed in the sky and the heat of the day began.

The two horses could then have a well-earned rest until the evening when probably there might be another field to be swath turned. For this Dad or one of the men used the white horse, General, who was a loner and worked on his own, never in a team.

24

Peg and I liked to watch the horses circling the field, the tall grass falling in neat rows. One year Wansdyke was ploughed up and corn planted there instead of the usual hay crop. We watched the cutting of this from the bottom gateway. Gradually the circle of corn got smaller and smaller until the rabbits and field mice, trapped in this ever diminishing sanctuary and fearing the blades of the knives, bolted for the hedge. Unseen by us, some of the boys from the village with sticks and two dogs came through the gateway of Old Pond Field. They chased and bludgeoned to death several of these unfortunate creatures, whilst the two dogs caught and killed a few more of them. Horrified, Peg and I were rooted to the spot unable to turn away or even to shut our eyes and ears to what seemed to us the most horrific scene. Sadly, we made our way home, the glorious September day spoiled for us before it had hardly begun. It was a long time before we could forget this or realise that it was quite a commonplace happening in the country. In the future we made sure that we were not around for this so called sport.

It was always a worrying time when the hay was nearly fit to be carried and the weather was unsettled. There was always the danger that it would be put in the rick green and then later it might heat up and eventually ignite. When it was a dry spell and there were no such problems, the general air of good humour spread to us children and we revelled in this feeling of well being. The men on the load flung the hay in the bottom of the elevator and joked with the two on the rick. Frolic, the pony, trod her monotonous circle working the machinery of the elevator, sometimes slowing down to such an extent that the steep mountain of sweetly smelling hay was hardly moving.

"Gee up there, Frolic." Dad would call from the top of the rick and the young pony would practically break into a trot so the rick makers were almost buried as they strove to move the heavy hay from the centre of the rick to the outside.

We watched as load after load came into the rick-yard and the stack got higher and higher. Dad would come down from the rick and replenish the old stone cider jar from the barrel in the dairy and the empty wagons creaked as they left for the hayfield. The drier the weather the more noise they seemed to make. The sun went down from a red sky which promised another such day tomorrow.

When it was a wet season, however, the new grass grew through the swathes of soggy hay as it lay on the ground for weeks. That which was nearly fit was cocked into mounds all over the field but in the persistent rain the water seeped through, spoiling the crop. When it was eventually carried the hay was dark and dusty.

As the relentless rain beat against the farm windows and the water butt at the end of the house overflowed into the yard, some of the despair of the grownups rubbed off onto Peg and me and we felt miserable. Eventually, of course, the clouds would clear and some of the crop would be saved, but it would be what old village folk described as "A caddling time".

In 1926, during or just after the General Strike, we had a young out-of-work miner to help on the farm.

Ron quickly established himself as a great favourite with Peg and me — we loved him dearly, spending all the time we could with him whilst he was at his farm work. We sat on the curved sides of the empty wagon and rattled over the bumpy ground to the haymaking field with Ron leading the horse. If we were lucky we got a lift back to the rick-yard, on top of the load of hay bowing our heads when Bonny and Trooper thundered through the gateway of Moremead to avoid the overhanging elm branches. We went with Ron to feed the young cattle in the Long Ground, riding back in the empty tip-up cart afterwards. Sometimes we stood on the bed of the cart, peering out over the high head board, pretending we were pigs on the way to market or otherwise sitting on the floor of the cart, where all we could see were the dark pitted boards smelling of cow cake and manure.

Ron had a fund of stories of life in the Somerset Coalfields — Midsomer Norton seemed miles away, to be another world in fact. We sat on the bottom rungs of the steps leading from the stables to the hayloft, whilst Ron was cleaning the harness and thought how wonderful it would be if he could stay at the farm for ever and not go back the mines. If we pleaded with him Ron would sing "*Two Little Girls in Blue*" in his soft Somerset accent. I don't know if that song was his entire repertoire but that was the only song we really wanted to hear — we were convinced that he had written the words himself, just for us.

In the summer Ron followed the fairs around — he was an expert at the ~~coconut shies~~ and always came away with a prize. His bedroom in the small cottage where he had lodgings was full of china ornaments, plates, glass etc. and was a veritable Aladdin's Cave. When he had a Sunday off he spent his day cleaning and shining his trophies. However the time came when Ron returned to the pits and Peg and I wept at losing him. We thought of his face, brown from the summer's sun, growing pale from long hours down the mines and we shed fresh tears for him.

Mother's hens seemed to be scattered all over the farm with hen houses and small units of poultry in all the furthest fields. There were generally young pullets feeding on the stubble in Wansdyke, a couple of hen houses in Old Pond Field and an isolated tumble-down one in Jack Daw. On the other side of the road, there were some in the field behind the Orchard, not counting the young half grown birds which started off in a large house in the Home Field.

It was quite a work letting them all out in the morning and giving them their morning feed. Then someone had to return in the afternoon with more corn to collect the eggs. This meant remembering to bring the keys of the hen houses — an enormous bunch tied to an old cow's horn with knotted string grown thick and greasy with constant handling. There must have been keys on the bunch which belonged to houses long since obsolete. Mother knew all the various keys but when Peg and I undertook the feeding on our own, we had to try lots of keys before hitting on the right one.

The keys normally hung on a large nail on the cobwebby wall of the granary. Sometimes they got

28

mislaid, which meant a frantic search by the entire family and, one dreadful afternoon, we dropped them into the brook which bordered Jack Daw. Crossing the narrow wooden bridge and swinging the empty egg basket between us, there was a sickening plop and we saw the cow's horn and the keys being swept rapidly downstream. Luckily they got caught up in the reeds at the foot of an old willow tree and we retrieved them with a hooked stick.

When one eventually got into the hen house there was always the hazard of broody hens to contend with. They would sit firmly in the nest box which held the most eggs and peck furiously at anyone trying to dislodge them. The secret was to pull them off firmly and quickly before they had the chance to break any of the eggs they were covering. Broodies had to be reported to Mother who would shut them away on their own until they lost their maternal instincts and recommenced laying.

"Penning up the hens" seemed to rule our social life. It entirely governed the length of time we could be away from home. Visits had to be cut short so that at dusk the shutters could be pegged down in the trap doors, and the poultry made safe for the night and from marauding foxes. One couldn't be too premature in "penning up the hens" either because there always seemed to be one hen perched indecisively on the steps of the trap door, unwilling to join the others inside. If she caught sight of anyone approaching she would run to meet them joyfully and nine times out of ten the others would join her expecting a late evening meal. It was by far the best plan to stay hidden until her head at least was safely inside the house and then dash forward and push the shutter home.

The pond was just outside the rick-yard, bounded on one side by the Home Ground with the further bank was in the Orchard. Normally there was always water there varying in depth according to the season. Mother kept Khaki Campbell ducks. They would be hatched under broody hens and, for the first week or so of their lives, they would be quite happy in the rick-yard — the mother hen scratching up the odd worm for them and cluck-clucking and fussing over them. Then they would find the pond and were soon swimming from one bank to another, whilst the old hen would rush up and down in a great state.

Eventually the ducklings grew up and were moved to the duck house by the pigsty wall. They always had to be left in their houses until mid-morning as they laid their pale green eggs in the early part of the day and, if loose, one had to search for them amongst the stinging nettles.

Perhaps because of their late start to the day, they were never very keen to go into their house at night, preferring to stay on the pond, idly swimming up and down in the half-light. We would stand on the orchard bank and try to drive them off, but sometimes they were very stubborn and ignored us. On one occasion Mother, losing patience, took off her shoes and stockings and waded into the pond. This took them so by surprise, that they made for their house, quacking loudly, stumbling through the trap door on their ungainly feet.

The gleanies (guinea fowls) were also a problem at "shutting up" time. They scorned the perches in their dry little fowl house and preferred to roost in the highest elm tree they could find. I don't really know why Mother kept them as we rarely found their small delicious eggs. They were, however, wonderful watchdogs and their raucous cries of "Go back! Go back!" would warn us of the approach of any stranger. At night Mother would spend a long time trying to shake the branch they were roosting on by means of a long stick. Quite often they would fly down, only to soar upwards immediately to a higher branch of another tree.

All would have been well if they had stayed in the tree until it was daylight but, unlike the ducks, they were early risers and were then a prey to any marauding fox.

Foxes were a problem to us. As tenant farmers and living in the midst of the Avon Vale hunting country Dad was not allowed to shoot a fox. In fact, if found doing so we could have been turned out of the farm, although I don't suppose Lord Landsdowne would have gone to such drastic lengths. If by any chance one lost stock through the fox, provided one could prove that reasonable care had been taken to safeguard it, compensation would be paid by the hunt. It was a rather lengthy drawn out business, involving someone inspecting the dead birds and the sum paid out never really seemed adequate to cover the cost of rearing and looking after the hens. Mother once discovered a fox with one of her best ducks in its mouth. It was a large dog fox, but Mother bravely chased it into one of the sheds, where it dropped the duck unhurt. Cornered, it turned and bared its teeth at Mother before it ran off into the fields. We thought this was very brave on the part of little Mother.

Soon after this Dad discovered another fox about to kill some of Mother's best layers in the middle of the afternoon and he shot it. All would have been well if he had buried it immediately but Vic Paget wanted the skin. I think he was courting strongly at the time and thought he would cure the skin and make a nice fur as a present for his young lady. The fox was put in a sack in the cart shed, where Barbara discovered it. Dad and Vic must have underestimated her intelligence by telling her that it was "a poor dead dog".

"They must think I'm daft," she told Peg and Me. "I've never yet seen a dog with a brush and a mask." As we all knew now, we all had to be sworn to secrecy.

For a while after this, Peg and I thought it highly probably that Dad's deadly sin would be found out. We had visions of our exodus from the farm, Dad driving the cows, Mother leading the horses, the wagons in much the same way as gypsies travelled with their bantams. We reckoned on the gleanies causing no end of problems.

Every year Mother reared turkeys, hatching the eggs under broody hens. Quite a few of the eggs would turn out to be infertile but the others thrived with their foster mothers.

It was when they were older that the difficulties started. They had a coop and a run on the little lawn outside one of the dining room windows, and every care was lavished on them but the turkey poults (a young turkey or fowl) seemed to have a very decided death wish. In a heavy storm, they would huddle in their run, scorning their warm coop, until their feathers clung to their thin bodies and they caught colds. When it was hot they sat in the full glare of the midday sun until they had to be revived by sips of water administered to them in the shade. Mother would spend ages chopping up hard-boiled eggs, lettuce and salad for their food but they still ate the long grass of their runs until they nearly choked. They suffered from black head, the gapes and coxcidiosis, but amazingly enough a few survived until Christmas.

Although there were so many chores to be done on the farm, there was also so much work to be done in our large inconvenient home.

Washing day at the farm was quite a ritual. Mother rose early to fill the fire box in the large copper with lighting wood. When this was well alight, coal was added and then the water was soon warm enough for some of it to be ladled into large tin baths and a start could be made on the clothes.

The washing fell into three categories — "the whites", "the coloured things" and "the rough things". If the coloured could be finished and pegged out with the whites in the morning, then all was going well. The clothes billowed out in the breeze and, if Mother was lucky, when she had finished hanging out the milking smocks, rough towels etc., some of the thinner things were dry. However, sometimes lunch had come and gone before the wicker basket full of coloured things had had their final rinse. Then, in spite of being put through the heavy mangle, the clothes hung dismally on the line, flapping disconsolately. It seemed evening before Mother was swilling down the brick shed with the soapy "suds" and the smell of soap permeated the house until bedtime.

Monday was the day that faggots were made at the little village shop. This fitted in very well with the busy day at home. Peg and I, complete with basin, were sent up there to buy some for the midday meal. They were delicious, made from home produced pork by Mrs Hunt, the shopkeeper wife of a butcher. The shop at Stockley must have been one of the smallest in the country. Two large sweet jars would fill the minute window and there was hardly room for portly Mrs Little, Mrs Hunt's mother, to stand behind the small counter.

Mrs Hunt stocked Dad's brand of tobacco and he would send Peg and me there once a week for a fresh supply. Besides the tobacco, he would have his week's ration of throat lozenges — little tiny black liquorice ones. The correct name for them escapes me now, as it must have done Dad on one occasion.

"Two ounces of Afrikender tobacco for Daddy, please, Mrs Little," I said. "And an ounce of those little black devils," added Peg firmly.

If Mrs Little was either amused or shocked, it didn't show on her good-natured face.

Not a great deal of time was taken up by shopping however, as most things were delivered to the door.

Besides Wiltshires from Calne, who delivered our groceries in a red painted delivery van once a week, there were several callers.

Alfie Summers was the fish merchant from Pewsham and he called on Fridays. I think the farm must have been one of the last calls of the day on his long round. In the winter, it was dark before he arrived and he always seemed depressed. His horse, too, drooped sadly in the shafts. Mother would go out to inspect his fish and fruit by the flickering light of a candle lantern.

"I've got a nice bit of filleted 'addock," he would inform Mother sadly, but he didn't sound at all pleased about it. In fact you'd think he was telling her of some dread disease he had developed.

Mother would perhaps buy cherries when they were in season or sometimes a watermelon as a special treat. The fish was quite good also, although one would wonder how it could keep fresh in that jolting cart in the summer's heat and dust.

Alfie Holmes was the village carrier, he lived with his widowed mother at Heddington Wick. He was a dwarf, little more than four feet tall, and Peg and I would measure ourselves by him, standing back to back to his stocky little frame. Gradually I got as tall, then Peg did, and eventually we could both look down on him. He didn't seem to mind these comparisons. Alfie would call for Mother's eggs and take them to Devizes market — swinging himself up to the driving seat of this high carrier's cart by his strong arms. In comparison to his size, the horse and cart seemed enormous but he manipulated them both very well.

Mr Knott sold paraffin, oil, candles etc. and he would call each fortnight. I don't know if he had been injured during the Great War but he had an artificial nose, which gave his face an unusual flat appearance, and his voice was hoarse and guttural. Mother bought oil and wicks for the lamps from him. He had many other wares, packed tight on shelves in his large covered van. High mounds of Windsor soap stood next to washing soda and squares of blue, blacklead, Brasso and bleach besides many different sorts of boot polish. There were all sorts of lamps, from the very smallest with minute wicks to large brass ones with fat bulging globes. On the back of the van was the paraffin drum complete with tap and round the sides hung mops, brushes and kettles.

CHAPTER
FOUR

The Village

The parc

Stockley Hollow was, and still is, one of the prettiest parts of the village. Its narrow chalk lane, fairly level to start with, rose steeply between high banks of meadowsweet.

Halfway along the steepest part of the lane was the old garden. It had at one time belonged to a thatched cottage, destroyed by fire at the beginning of the last century. Freddie Summers, from West View Cottages at the bottom of the Hollow, rented this patch of land as an allotment.

Peg and I would always stop and look through the wicket gate set in the high hedge. The old well was still there, along with a bullace (wild plum) tree and some lilac bushes. As well as cultivating the land as a vegetable garden, Freddie grew a border of flowers, edged by a wide grass path. In fact the whole garden looked very unlike an allotment. The green path, curving round the rose trees in the distance, looked as if it should lead right up to a cottage door.

We weaved stories about that non-existent cottage and wished that someone would build a house to fit in that beautiful garden, so that children could swing in the bullace tree and race down the neat path into the leafy lane.

When spring came Freddie would often be raking down the soil for a seedbed whilst primroses bloomed in the bank outside the neatly trimmed hedge and daisies and polyanthus line the grass path inside. In the late summer he would be digging the potatoes out in rows on the dark soil; the borders would then be ablaze with dahlias. Quite often he would be tending his own patch at home, then the garden would be deserted, slumbering in the sun — only the wood pigeons calling from the woods and the lazy sounds of the bees breaking the silence.

The Hollow continued on past the disused chalk quarry until we were in Violet Lane. I think we must have bestowed this name upon this particular part of the Hollow. Here in the spring the high banks were coloured by quantities of deep blue dog violets and the smaller sweetly scented white variety. The hazel branches met overhead, forming a dense ceiling and blotting out the sunshine until one reached the wooden gate and the open countryside once more.

The Blackland Golf Club was on the other side of the road. It stretched across undulating countryside, its hollows and slight hills forming natural bunkers. Peg and I would spend a long time there hunting for stray golf balls in the rough grass. Sometimes I think we found the balls before they were actually lost. Many a plus-foured player must have hunted in vain for his errant ball whilst it was safely tucked away up one of our knicker legs.

Quite often the afternoon slipped away too quickly and, warned by the lengthening shadows, we would make for home. Once we asked a lone golfer if he could tell us the time, plucking up enough courage while he was selecting a club for his next shot. He produced a large "Turnip" watch from the inside of his golf jacket and proceeded to explain the elementary process of telling the time. We at last managed to get away delayed by all this unnecessary instruction.

"We knew how to tell the time years ago." said Peg, as we ran over the field and climbed the gate into Violet Lane.

To the right of the Hollow was a cornfield, splashed with the scarlet of poppies at Harvest time, and beyond that were the woods — Stockley and Blackland Woods, separated from each other by a narrow field. We knew Stockley Wood well, each little drive which led off the main track through the trees. We knew where to find the best bluebells in May and where to find the little clearing which was golden with lent lilies at Easter time.

We were somewhat afraid of Jimmy Vines who was the gamekeeper for the Bowood Estates and was often to be found in the woods. He rode a bike to and from his cottage at Heddington. There always seemed to be a bundle of pea or bean sticks tied to the crossbar, whatever the season. He consequently cycled slowly and ponderously, his knees stuck out at a peculiar angle.

Blackland Woods, on the other hand, were a mystery to us, we rarely ventured into them. Occasionally we would go to the edge of the tall trees and peer into the green, cool darkness but we'd soon return to the friendly shelter of our own woods. We loved them at all seasons, in the spring when the wood anemones sprinkled the ground like fallen stars, through the heat of a midsummer day when the honeysuckle clambered through the thicket, trying to reach the sun's rays. They even seemed attractive on a winter's day when the trees were bare of leaves and frost laced the undergrowth with silver.

When we were all quite young, Mother would drive us all to church in the pony tub. This must have been quite a lengthy procedure. The horse had first to be harnessed to the tub, we then trotted all through the village, past the Ivy Inn to Lower Farm, where we all dismounted. Here Mother had an arrangement whereby the horse spent the time we were in church in one of their stables.

We generally reached Lower Farm just as the five-minute bell started, so we would take the short cut to the church over the Manor Orchard. The iron gate at the other end opened onto the road just opposite the lych-gate. Afterwards, of course, the whole procedure was re-enacted in reverse, Mother harnessed up the horse and we trotted home.

When we were older and some of the family had bikes, we didn't use the tub. On foot, bike or pillion, we arrived at church by various means and at various times. Those arriving first spread themselves out to forestall interlopers so that the family could eventually sit together.

40

"Our" pew was divided three parts of the way down by a wide stone pillar. When we all attended, plus perhaps a visitor or so, two had to "sit behind the pillar". This had its advantages and disadvantages. One could fidget without a disapproving poke from Mother, or lean sideways or backwards and read a few of the visible tablets on the walls. This filled in a little time if the sermon proved long or uninteresting. On the other hand one's view of the rest of the church was very limited. When one knelt one could just see Albert Grey pumping the organ handle up and down — sometimes he would forget to start those essential few seconds before the beginning of a hymn. The organist would then get off to a wheezy start for the first few bars. We could just see the pulpit, but not the lectern, and the men's choir in the chancel was completely hidden from view.

Peg and I liked the children's service, held once a month, especially when there was an extra special one such as a Harvest Gift service or one on Easter Sunday. Then the church was bright with spring flowers and the pillar in "our" pew was garlanded with primroses that we had picked in Stockley Wood.

Good Friday was an odd sad day. Mother would normally play the organ for the three hours service. I think it was the only time in the year that she was called upon to do so — I suppose the hours — noon till three o'clock in the afternoon — was an awkward time for the regular organist. Peg and I accompanied her once.

"Stay for half an hour or so and go out during one of the hymns." instructed Mother. "It will be quite alright as other people will be doing the same thing."

Half an hour or so elapsed, but we thought we'd better not appear too eager to be gone, so we decided to wait until the next hymn. This proved to be quite a short one and we were scared we'd left it too late and would be struggling with the heavy oak door when the prayers started again. The next hymn was "*Forty days and forty nights*" — we rather liked this one and thought we'd stay and join in. The next suitable time, nobody left and we didn't want to leave on our own. And so it went on. Mother, getting anxious, leaned around on the organ stool and noiselessly mouthed "Go out when you like," in the middle of the rendering of "*Christian does Thou see them*", but by this time we thought we might as well stay to the bitter end. It seemed as if we had been there for at least a day, and the bright spring sunshine seemed strange after the cool shade of the church.

Walking home to the usual Good Friday meal of boiled haddock, Peg and I decided that we could not possibly ever become nuns. We felt that life in a convent would be like a lifetime of the Three-Hour Services.

Immediately in front of "our" pew, sat Mrs Clifton, the Rector's wife, and her beautiful daughter, Jessie. At least Peg and I thought Jessie was beautiful — she had spent years abroad and was always elegantly dressed and her perfume was exotic; waves of it wafted back to us in church.

She drove the family car — a solid wheeled Trojan, whose engine had a very distinctive sound. Hearing its approach from afar, Peg and I would rush to the garden gate and look out as it chugged by — Miss Clifton at the wheel with her father beside her, whilst Mrs Clifton sat regally in the back seat. We would wave and they would wave back. Once on rushing to the gate a Brooke Bond Divi Van drove by, vanishing in a cloud of dust up the road. We were very taken aback, we thought that a Trojan engine was unique to the Clifton family.

There was one occasion in church when Miss Clifton would have been forgiven for losing her "cool". In the Manor Orchard was a large sweet chestnut tree and Barbara had collected some chestnuts *en route* for the morning service one autumn day. She was wearing a coat with wide fur cuffs and put these chestnuts inside them for safekeeping. All went well until the closing hymn and the collection. Forgetting that the chestnuts were there, she lifted her arms to put her coppers in the bag and the whole lot shot onto the floor. Some landed on the Rectory pew, ricocheting off the polished wood into the aisle, others slid along the book rest and crashed onto the floor with a sound like a machine gun fire.

Without a backward glance, Miss Clifton never faltered in the singing of the hymn, one neatly gloved hand holding her book in front of her beautiful impassive face.

Behind the church were the downs — we loved their peaceful beauty. Kings Play, in particular, was one of our favourite haunts. To get to it one walked nearly to

43

the top of Heddington Hollow and then cut across the rolling downlands. Here a multitude of wild flowers grew in profusion, all those beautiful one that are common to chalk land. Here we found the dainty blue harebell, wild mauve scabious and numerous sorts of orchids. The latter had to be searched for in the short grass. Bee and slipper orchids grew there and once we found the rare man orchid.

The dewponds were still in existence then. Peg and I always paid them a visit, marvelling at their ever-constant supply of drinking water for the sheep. The sheep roamed these hills and some of the leaders wore small tinkling bells. The sound of these, coupled with the song of the skylark and the mournful cry of the peewit, were all part of the summery scene.

Peg and I would sit on the summit of Kings Play and look down on Heddington and Stockley laid out in miniature before us, the ribbon of road winding through Heddington until it became the Stockley Road.

Some landmarks were easy to determine — the sombre dark shape of Bullocks Barn, contrasting with the paler softer shades of the fields around it. There were cows in the field between the Barn and Harley Lane — black and white Friesians, knee deep in buttercups. From the distance they looked like animals from a toy farm as they moved slowly to the watering place in the middle of the field, grazing as they went. It was this field that we christened "The Kingcup Field" because in the spring there was always a large clump of marsh marigolds on the edge of the pond.

Paddock Farm would stand out clearly down its long drive, but we couldn't see our own Stockley Farm, the trees in the neighbouring fields hid it from view. We could just see the roof of Willowbrook and then the rest of the village faded into a misty mixture of sky and trees, no other landmarks distinguishable.

To the side of Kings Play were the fox covers — a dark lonely shady place where the sun's rays rarely penetrated. We didn't linger here, but would set off home towards Stockley Hollow, passing the Shepherd's lonely house on the way. Situated in a valley between two hills, it looked sheltered and peaceful in the sunshine but would be a wild, bleak place in the winter. During a very hard spell, the snow would drift down into the valley, covering with a white blanket the twisted thorn bushes, misshapened by the wind. The old shepherd would occasionally come down into the village, but rarely ventured into Devizes or Calne and, so the locals said, had never travelled by train. He was a fund of information about all things connected with nature and his weather prophesies were more reliable than most.

Before we reached the Hollow, we went across the Toboggan Ridge — a grand name for an ordinary sloping field with a level few yards at the bottom. If the snow was thick enough in the winter, we would join forces with the Bryant boys from Bell Farm. I can't recall that we had a great deal to do with them for the rest of the year, but they owned this magnificent toboggan which would hold ten children with ease. It was most beautifully built. It was however, extremely heavy and took all the older children much time and effort to haul it up the slope. Peg and I were, I think, used as ballast on the way down, squeezed in between the bigger passengers. We'd start off slowly, keeping a straight course but as the toboggan gradually gathered speed, some of the children would be dislodged and in the end the few surviving passengers would be desperately trying to gain control of the careering sledge, which would eventually come to rest in a snowdrift.

On a summer's day sitting on the warm turf at the top of the ridge, it all looked so different. The slope, which seemed so precipitately steep on a snowy January afternoon, now looked so gentle.

When we eventually had bikes, the round trip from Stockley to Heddington and back took us quite a long time, as there were quite a few hills to negotiate.

Where parts of the village around the church, with our beloved downs behind, always seemed to be bathed in light and sunshine, the other end of the village took on a more sombre appearance. The common, in particular, appeared a gloomy place with its scattering of cottages, goats and tethered animals grazing on the wide verges and a few hens scratching around in the dusty grass. Once a year the common would come into its own — that was, of course, when the Annual Flower Show took place in one of the neighbouring fields. Then there would be plenty of light and music.

One November afternoon, Peg and I were cycling along the road, wearing blue coats. Mother had sewn a width of fur around the hems — I'm not quite sure whether this was as an adornment or whether it was to lengthen them.

Jack Dixon lived on the common in a caravan and he had several dogs of the greyhound/whippet strain. I suppose he used them for rabbiting but quite a lot of the time they were tied up underneath the caravan, but on this particular occasion they were loose. Our cheap coney fur must have attracted their sporting instincts because they set off after our bikes with enthusiasm.

With them yapping at our heels, we raced down the little slope past the Wheelwright's, pedalling furiously by Prince Brown's Farm. The bullrushes in the pond opposite the farm were bent low in the autumn wind and by this time the daylight was fading. We must have reached Broad's Green before the dogs gave up the chase and slunked home. The danger past, we still carried on at the same speed until we reached the safety of our own yard.

One of our favourite expeditions was to walk from Heddington Wick to Turnpike Farm and from there to Beacon Hill. Beacon Hill was the old coach road from Bath. It was very steep in places and apparently years ago, oxen were kept in the village and were used to pull the carriages up the steepest part. A cottage had once stood where the road forked to Hitchen Lane and the man who lived there had the job of unhitching the teams of horses and replacing them with the oxen.

The high banks of the old chalk road were scattered with ragged gorse bushes and our vivid imagination took control. We thought we heard the creaking of the gibbet on the evening air and was it or was it not the sound of carriage wheel in the distance?

Our plimsolls sliding on the wet chalk, we scrambled down the last few yards of track and eventually reached Pig Lane. There the reassuring light of the oil lamp from Annie Summer's cottage and the shadowy outlines of her tethered goats, feeding on the side of the road, brought us back to normality once more.

CHAPTER
FIVE

Friends and Neighbours

Dad had taken over the farm in 1903 and during his bachelor years, Joshiah Gregory and his wife lived in the farmhouse. Mrs Gregory was the housekeeper and Joshiah worked on the farm. When Dad married they retired and went to live in a little cottage in Stockley.

We often visited them in their little thatched home — the garden looking its best in late summer, when the borders were filled with brightly coloured phlox. Mrs Gregory, standing at the gate with her white hair and dressed in an old fashioned wrap-around print apron, blended in with the colour scheme.

Mrs Gregory would never admit to being completely fit — always "middling", never "fair to middling". The fact that she lived to be over 100 years rather belied this.

Dad had many anecdotes to tell about old Joshiah. One of Joshiah's jobs on the farm was to drive the milk float into Calne, loaded with the day's milk in churns. Several times he'd arrive back at the farm on a winter's night and he would have forgotten to light the candle lamps in front of the float. Dad apparently got quite cross when, after repeatedly telling Joshiah about this, one blustery December night he heard the approaching milk float but still no light visible.

"Whatever are you at, Joshiah, you've forgotten to light those candles again!" said Dad.

"No, I ain't forgot, Gaffer, they'm lit alright but I 'ad to tie some sacking round 'em cus the wind kept blowing of 'em out," retorted Joshiah.

Joshiah's memory seems to be have been quite a worry to him. Apparently he would wander around, saying to himself, "If only I could remember where I 'ad it last!"

Tom Paget and his wife lived in the furthest cottage in the rank about a quarter of a mile from the farm. They had for years lived in the lone cottage up Stockley Hollow, where they had raised their large family of thirteen. The cottage was burnt to the ground and only the garden remained.

When Peg and I were children, Tom had already retired from full time work at the farm, although I believe one of the sons still worked there. Tom would do a few hours a day, mostly in the garden.

Gardening was his hobby and he was certainly an expert at it. Mother delivered the Parish Magazine once a month to several houses in Stockley and the Pagets were on her list. The visit to their cottage was always a joy. The kitchen with its glowing fireirons, the range blackleaded till it shone and the mantelshelf alive with china animals on its tasselled red baize cover. The stone floor was scrubbed white and there were gaily-coloured rag rugs. Their old horned gramophone was generally playing "*How Sweet the Name of Jesus Sounds*" as befitted a Sunday afternoon.

The visit always followed the same pattern — Peg and I enduring the pleasantries that preceded Tom's "Be coming down the garden?" as he reached for his hat. I supposed there must have been failures in that garden but to Peg and me, it all looked perfect — row after row of neat vegetables, well strung beans and lettuce always just right for cutting, the apple trees hung with rosy fruit which never seemed to be rotten or misshapen. On we marched single file down the narrow neatly cropped grass path, till we reached the end and look back in admiration. Skirting the marrow bed at the end, we started the walk back and there always seemed to be something fresh to admire, something we had missed the first time around.

In the cool kitchen once more, there was still another pleasure to come because Tom brewed his own wine and beautiful wine it was too. Before the days of fermentation vessels, airlocks, Camden tablets and what-have-you, his methods must have been simple by today's standards, but I should love to equal the excellence of the potato wine which we drank on those summer afternoons. At the age of six, Peg and I were quite confirmed wine tasters.

Both Tom and his wife had a fund of stories which we never tired of hearing. We loved to hear how Mrs Paget would walk from the cottage in Stockley Hollow to help with the day's wash at Rough Leaze Farm. She started work at 7.00a.m. and finished at dusk, coming home via Blackland Woods. Her pay was one shilling and sixpence (about 8p in today's money) a day plus a meal of bread, cheese and beer. We wondered how she could possibly cope with her large family after a day like that.

A rather uncanny story was the one concerning her pig. At the beginning of the last century, all cottages had a pig sty and I suppose pork from their own pig was their only meat for the winter. One summer day, Mrs Paget was feeding the pig when it jumped up and hit the bucket out of her hand, putting her thumb out of joint. It remained painful all the summer. (I suppose there was no money for doctor's fees for anything as trivial as that.) In the autumn the pig was killed and as Mrs Paget was salting the joints her thumb just slipped back into place once more.

Another visit to Mother's Parish Magazine list was to Auntie Edie's small house at Stockley. Auntie Edie and Uncle Harry had once lived at Lower Farm, Heddington, but, having fallen on bad times, retired to a newly built council house at Stockley.

It must have taken quite a lot of getting used to, this downward trend to their fortunes, but somehow Auntie Edie managed to bestow a little of her former grandeur to her small home. For instance, we were always received in the small front room, which was re-labelled "the drawing room", while the living room at the back bore the exalted name of "the dining room".

Auntie Edie was tall, thin and elegant. She rode on an old fashioned bike which always seemed more upright than any at the farm, probably because the saddle was higher. In the front of her bike was a little wicker basket in which rode Pixie, the Pekinese dog. Auntie Edie lavished a great deal of affection on Pixie, which perhaps accounted for her being extremely bad-tempered. I think she was quite capable of jumping out of the basket, all ready to start a fight if another dog met them on their bicycling expeditions. In fact Pixie, with her bulging eyes and snuffling nose, would tackle anything, safe I believe in the knowledge that she would be snatched to safety to Auntie Edie's bony bosom before any harm could come to her.

Uncle Harry was also a dedicated cyclist. When past seventy, he cycled to Cardiff on one occasion and all the way to Middlesex on another. His cycling outfit was a large cape and on his head he wore a tweed deerstalker type hat. Come to think of it, one never saw Auntie Edie and Uncle Harry cycling together. Even to church, Uncle Harry rode on in advance for his role of chief tenor in the Choir.

Auntie Edie had a close friend, Miss Roynon from Mile Elm, Calne, who drove a two-seater car with a dickie seat at the back. If we were lucky, Peg and I would get a ride in this seat, which was a great treat. There was one drawback however, Miss Roynon had never learnt to reverse the car. This would mean going miles out of the way to get on the right road or, worse still, enlisting the help of casual passers-by to reverse the jalopy for her. In the early nineteen twenties it was amazing the number of people who had to be approached before she was lucky enough to settle for a car driver. Peg and I sat in the dickie seat, dressed in our best clothes wearing our hats with the daisies on the brims, and squirmed with embarrassment. It was all so humiliating and spoilt a lovely outing. However, I don't think the indignity filtered through to Miss Roynon. When waved on by a policeman she had been known to call out "Do you wish me to proceed?" in a strident voice. However, many times she managed the trip to Burnham, travelling all through Bristol with all the hazards of the traffic and the tramlines,

Bill Bridges was a bachelor who lived at Broad's Green Farm with his parents. He drove an open Scout car with brass lamps — I think he must have driven it very badly or else he was accident prone, because there always seemed to be loads of incidents connected with his driving.

There was the time he gave the Ruddle boys a lift from Calne and took Ebor Cottage Corner too fast and the brothers landed in the hedge. It must have been a very prickly hedge because it took a long, long time to get all the thorns out of various parts of their anatomy.

One winter Saturday night, however, Bill thought it was far too icy on the roads for motor transport, so he walked the three miles into Calne to get the Sunday joint. Coming out of Hawkins with the meat, he met Pete Smith from Heddington, who had chanced the roads on his motor bike. Bill was persuaded, much against his better judgement, to accept a lift back home.

He first fell off at Mile Elm but, clutching his meat, remounted the pillion again, only to hit the deck once more at Weaver's Bridge and the joint landed in the muddy waters of the brook. Peering into the stagnant water they could just make out the sirloin trapped between a couple of fallen logs.

Bill hurried to the farm and got a rake and a prong and after a great deal of trouble managed to retrieve the Sunday lunch. Furtively he went into the kitchen of the farm and washed the soggy joint under the tap.

The next day he made some excuse and refused any of the offending joint but his parents were supposed to have said, "It was the best bit of beef they'd tasted for a long while". What they said when Bill told them from whence it had been rescued, is not recorded.

In our childhood eyes Willowbrook Farm was as beautiful as its name suggested. There lived our friends and neighbours — the Ruddle family. Mrs Ruddle was plump and rosy and baked the most delicious bread. I don't know how often she baked but the aroma of the home made bread always seemed to fill the old-fashioned kitchen and dairy. Peg and I, on visits to their farm, were allowed to try our hand at making tiny loaves and with great pride trotted home with them afterwards.

The Ruddle children were grown up — Bill, John and Maggie, who worked on the farm, and Jim who rode his motor bike into Calne each day to work. Flower Ruddle, the father, was plump and florid and rode a tricycle. This frightened Peg and me very much. I think it had little or no brakes, because Flower was unable to dismount on his own. After a trip out, he would wait until he reached our farm and then start ringing his bell continuously until Maggie would appear at their front gate, just in time to help father dismount. Fascinated, we would watch from behind our cowyard wall. We felt that there must be a time when Maggie would be unable to answer the parental summons. What if she was hanging out the clothes in the orchard or feeding the fowls in the rick-yard? Would Flower then vanish out of sight into the distance and be forced to tricycle the two miles around the village and attempt another landing? But Maggie was always there waiting, at least she was all the times we were watching.

The Ruddles had a servant called Clara. I believe she had once been in the local workhouse and I don't imagine she had any near relatives. Poor Clara was deaf and dumb but, in spite of this handicap, she managed to lead a very useful life. She used a kind of deaf sign language understood quite well by all the Ruddle family and they could talk back to her in the same way.

Sometimes when Mother was very busy, she was loaned Clara for the day. Peg and I thought her a fascinating person — we tried hard to copy the grownups with the sign language and this amused Clara very much. She would laugh, rocking backwards and forwards on her small black-booted feet, her long grey skirt swinging round her short legs.

For several years the Ruddles had a tennis court in the field behind their orchard — the field that bordered our land. I don't think it was a very grand court, just meadow grass rolled and mowed until it was smooth, with some rather tatty matting to catch the balls. It held great fascination for Peg and me, however. We would sit in the dry ditch of Jack Daw, screened by hazel twigs and dog roses, and watch the evening's play. It all seemed so romantic — Jim Ruddle and a couple of the men even sported white flannels and the girls in their short white tennis frocks and bobbed hair seemed to be straight out of a Noël Coward play. There cries of "Hard luck, partner!" or "Well played!" and much laughter and chat, while the gramophone churned out the latest hits from the sidelines.

As each set ended the players gathered perilously close to our hiding place for glasses of Eiffel Tower lemonade. Not daring to speak, we crouched low amongst the cow parsley and drank in that exciting scene. "*Old Man River*" replaced "*The Desert Song*" and play was resumed once more.

With desperate impatience of the very young, we willed the time to pass quickly so that we could be part of that exciting scene. Little did we know that in just over a decade, the war clouds would have gathered over Europe once more, Willowbrook full of evacuees and the tennis court ploughed up.

CHAPTER
SIX

The Seasons

We should have had great difficulty in deciding which was our favourite season — each in turn brought its own pleasures. I suppose the spring had more magic than the others.

There was always seemed to be one day in particular when the sun felt really warm for the first time that year; the banks were suddenly ablaze with golden celandines and, if one hunted, the primroses could be found in the long grass bordering the hedges. Even the birds were fooled and sung loud and long as they built under the eaves of the farmhouse. There would be one large clump of daffodils in the orchard, under the old Blenheim tree, and early wallflowers would scent the flower border. Winter would no doubt return later with cold winds and maybe snow but, just for that one magical day, it seemed to have gone for good.

Old Paget, trying to beat the heavy, dark clay soil of our vegetable garden down to a fine tilth for a seedbed, would gloomily mutter about the blackthorn winter which was sure to come. Peg and I, sitting with our backs against the boles of the fir trees, were convinced that he was wrong. The scent of hyacinths would waft through the open drawing room window — hyacinths that should have bloomed during the depth of winter but always seemed to wait for the first sunny warm days for their blue, pink and white blossoms to open.

It was during the spring that Mother used the incubator. This was something quite new, a very modern invention after years of hatching clutches of eggs under patient broody hens. The incubator with its oil lamp to provide the necessary warmth and its tray with setting eggs neatly laid out in rows was housed in the back kitchen. For three weeks Mother damped and turned the eggs daily and also inspected them for any addled or infertile ones. Then one day the tray would be alive with hatching chicks. Peg and I thought it was wonderful. Some of the first to be hatched would be dry, fluffy and attractive, as they pecked amongst the broken shells. Some would have damp feathers plastered against their grotesque little bodies, as they sprawled on the fine wire mesh, trying to raise the strength to get to their feet. Others would still be in their shells, just a small head with a questing beak showing through a tiny hole. The weaker ones would almost give up the struggle, lying motionless with closed eyes.

Mother would pick them up, hurry along the shed to the kitchen and hold them for a few moments in the smoke from the range. Nine times out of ten this would revive them — we could never understand why. We felt sure that anything so small and so near death would be asphyxiated by the thick smoke. Until they got as strong as the others Mother would put them in a box covered with flannel in front of the fire. Here they would probably stay all night, every now and then giving little chirps much to the curiosity of the cats.

By rights the cats should have been accustomed to strangers in front of their fireside. Mother quite often reared baby pigs there. They would be the surplus ones from a large litter or weaklings that stood little chance of survival in a sty with their sturdier brothers or sisters. Here they had the warmth of the room plus that of the old stone hot water bottle and the two hourly feeds of milk and water from a feeding bottle. Quite a few survived, getting quite domesticated in the end, becoming very fond of the family and snuggling down at night in their box with, sometimes, a cat for company.

When the days began to draw out Mother would start the "Spring-Cleaning", beginning with the bedrooms and working downwards. Rugs and carpets were hung on the clothesline and whacked vigorously with carpet beaters, then pulled along the short grass of the lawn to remove the dust. Paintwork was rubbed down with vinegar and water and the bedroom ware had a soapy scrub before it was put back on the marble wash stands. Sometimes Mother did a spot of home decorating. This was rather difficult with the sloping walls and flaking ceilings, especially using patterned paper, as the patterns never met correctly, no matter how skilfully the paper was cut.

Downstairs it was easier to clean as all the furniture could be moved out onto the lawn. A dustsheet thrown over the old suite from the drawing room made an interesting tent for Peg and me to play in. When we got tired of that Mother would let us wash the picture frames and polish the glass with soft cloths. The cats loved the spring cleaning, leaping into every open drawer and exploring avidly each yard of unaccustomed space made available when the heavy furniture was moved around. Only Jack hated it, however, fearing some major upheaval of crisis, he would sit pathetically on the bare floorboards where his favourite chair normally rested.

Our birthday in March would be unpredictable as to the weather. Some years warm enough to play outside until dusk, other times it would be cold with a biting wind and one year there was a flurry of snow scudding across the yard until a fine white carpet spread around the back door. " good weather words

I remember one year when the weather was really glorious on our birthday. Joan Attwood, a second cousin, who often came to stay with Auntie Edie was at the farm for tea. Joan, whose parents were abroad, spent a lot of time with us. Peg and I thought she was very sophisticated and gay; she had travelled more that most girls of her age. Her topics of conversation even included boyfriends, which we found very intriguing!

After the birthday tea Peg and I had made up our minds to go primrosing in the woods, but for some unknown reason the whole family insisted that we should all listen to Children's Hour on the wireless first. With bad grace we did so feeling that every moment spent indoors missing the late afternoon was wasted. I believe the Uncle on Children's Hour that

61

afternoon was Uncle Mac and we were thrilled to bits when he announced our birthday followed by "Hullo Twins". He also told us the hiding place of a present — a beautiful china doll that we called June. Joan had organised the broadcast and the gift of June; she later made us a treasure cot for the newcomer. Although not being terribly fond of dolls, we got a lot a pleasure out of June, she was so elegant with her dimpled pink face surrounded by real hair.

Summer would merge with spring so that only the length of days made one realise that it was nearly midsummer.

Dad would sit on the lawn in a deck chair on Sunday evenings, his best straw hat pulled down over his eyes whilst he puffed away at his pipe. This straw hat always reappeared for the few summer months, sometimes he would sport a new one and the old one would be relegated for use in the hayfield, gradually becoming more and more yellow with the strong rays of the sun.

Peg and I would find that we were going to bed in broad daylight and waking up with the sun streaming through the casement windows. Sleep was elusive even with the curtains drawn tightly shutting out the light. The world outside seemed very wide-awake and attractive; the sound of wagons wheels on the road or laughter in the distance, even the clink of the watering cans on the asphalt path as Mother watered the front border in the cool of the evening. We wished we were up and dressed and part of the busy scene.

Haymaking of course could make or mar our pleasure of the summer months. August and September could be pleasant, relaxed months if all had gone well and the hay was made and was good.

In late summer there was, of course, always the Flower Show to which we looked forward with pleasure. We also had long walks to Hampsley and Heddington Hollow and Beacon Hill and we'd even get as far as Oliver's Camp occasionally.

Relations would come to tea, Mother getting out the silver teapot that dribbled slowly from out of its narrow spout. The hot water jug would bubble on the spirit lamp and a slight smell of methylated spirit would drift through the dining room.

Most years there would be a Church Fête at the Manor during the summer. Stalls would be laid out on the lawns and coloured bunting would be strung along the white railing which separated the garden from the Orchard. Cake stalls with a mouth-watering selection of home-made delicacies and a needlework stall with tablecloths, chair backs and antimacassars embroidered with coloured silks in a multitude of shades and designs, would be set up on the gravel in front of the windows.

Of course there would be a bran tub. Pushing one's hand and arm down into the dry bran, there was the agonising decision whether it was best to choose something small on the assumption that all the best things were in small parcels, or whether to plump for the biggest ones groping fingers could find. One year the Reverend Clifton's successor, Mr Teague, a dear saintly but impracticable rector, was given the task of buying gifts for the bran tub. Armed with the necessary money supplied by the Church Council he made his way to Woolworth's in Bath. There he seemed to make his way to all the wrong counters because he returned with the most unsuitable things. Firelighters and nutmegs in profusion but not a single toy or bag of sweets. I think kindly parishioners managed to provide a few things which were more suitable and these they mixed in with the others but there were quite a few disappointed children that afternoon.

Autumn would edge its way in before we had really appreciated the summer. The evenings would shorten and Mother would be obliged to light the lamps before suppertime. The big oil lamp that stood on the kitchen table would throw a yellow glow over the thick tablecloth but its light would never quite penetrate into the corners of the room.

There would be a tiny oil lamp on the wall where the front stairs curved round to the landing. This would flare, blackening the glass, when the back door was left open. Candles were used in the bedrooms, throwing grotesque shadows on the walls. The candles would burn unevenly and the hot wax would run down into the candlesticks forming miniature white stalactites. I once caught the lace curtains of our bedroom alight while reading in bed by the light of one of these guttering candles. I got severely told off by Mother — reading in bed, like reading by firelight, being bad for the eyes in Mother's estimation. The fire did no damage; Mother resourcefully rolled the burning curtains in the bedroom rug!

Later on the Aladdin Lamp was invented and we had two of those. The bright white light from them was far superior to the yellow glow from the old brass lamp. However, these didn't like draughts either and the mantles would blacken and alarming red and yellow flames would shoot up the chimney glass if the lamp was left in a current of air. When the wick was turned down the mantle gradually returned to normal and the lamp would burn steadily again, giving out a friendly little hum as it did so.

During October, the garden changed overnight, Mother taking up the last of the summer flowers to make way for the wallflowers. Peg and I followed behind her wheelbarrow and cut off the few remaining blooms of the asters and put their shaggy blossoms in paste pots and brought them indoors.

The chestnut trees lost their golden leaves and we scuffed our way through them in the Manor Orchard on the way to church.

The apples were picked in — red greasy-skinned Tom Putts, earthy-tasting Russets and my favourites, little hard-fleshed Pippins. The best ones were carried up to the box room shelves to store for the winter. There was one old pear tree in the corner of the orchard, which bore a multitude of small sweet pears. The tree was far too insecure to bear the weight of a ladder and the fruit had to be shaken down and then retrieved from the long grass. This fruit was always known as the "Boardy" pears — presumably because of their hardness and to distinguish them from the Williams pears on the end of the house, which were picked and put in drawers to ripen. If caught at the right time, they were delicious, but if left too long they became dark, sleepy and inedible.

November came with, occasionally, a touch of winter when there was a frost hard enough to lay ice in the cartruts in the gateways. Other days it would be mild and still with a temporary return to the mellow autumn weather.

We had a few fireworks each year, Dad letting them off in the shed while we watched from the back door. The squibs would shoot back and forth on the brick floor. Punch, Barbara's cat, unafraid and inquisitive, chasing after them until she was picked up by Mother who was afraid of her burning her paws. In high dudgeon she then sat on the saddle of Dick's bike, her twitching ears and swinging tail showing her resentment at these noisy, darting little interlopers.

Whatever the state of the finances, Mother would always have a studio photo of the four of us at least once every two years. This would generally take place in the autumn and then the finished photos could be posted around to the relatives at Christmas.

How we hated these long drawn out sessions at the Studios in Calne. The photographer was fussy to the extreme, always striving for perfection which I'm afraid was impossible with our family as subjects. Mother would have us all dressed in our best, Peg and I with our fringes freshly trimmed for the occasion. The studios were dimly it and full of peculiar "props" used for background purposes. As well as several large sofas and chairs, there were a few enormous slabs of stone and, in one of our photos, we are all posed in front of

66

one of these. Dick told Peg and me that these were really ~~tombstones~~ with the inscriptions rubbed off and this we steadfastly believed for years.

One year when the proofs arrived we were surprised to find ourselves disembodied, just our four heads appeared to float across the picture, our faces bearing rather startled expressions. The whole effect was rather ethereal but I don't think Mother thought she had got her money's worth.

As the days grew shorter, the night frost would be too severe for the rays of the winter sun to thaw out during the day and there would be prolonged periods when the ground was held in its icy grasp for weeks.

When there was snow we would renew our acquaintances with the Bryant boys and their magnificent sledge. When it was really thick, we would make a snowman on the lawn, using two pieces of coal for its bright glittering eyes. Completed, it would look quite lifelike with one of Dad's straw hats (discarded even for haymaking) set at a rakish angle on its head and a scarf tied tightly round its neck. Gradually as the thaw set in, its thickset body would slump, subsiding at last into a messy heap of discoloured slush.

One year the pond by the rick-yard froze hard enough to bear our weight. We all slid around it for days, creeping along by the bushes at the edge to start with and gradually summoning up enough courage to go from one bank to another.

Mother knitted Peg and me stocking caps with mittens to match. When the thick wool of the mittens got wet they were very uncomfortable and cold. We found it best to dig our bare hands deep down inside the pockets of our thick coats.

During the snowy time the hens would be even more trouble at shutting up time, thinking it wasn't yet bed time because of the bright glare from the drifts of snow. Even when a path was cleared for them to the trap door of the henhouse they still hesitated, scratching disconsolately with cold feet on the hard ground.

The evenings were long on these winter nights. One day Mother would light a fire in the dining room, the next in the drawing room ... "To air both rooms equally," she said. Consequently several nights a week we could crouch beside the large fireplace in the dining room while the wind whistled down the big chimney, every now and then sending billowing smoke out into the room. The wooden shutters would rattle at the windows and the heavy velvet curtains at the door never completely kept out the draughts. On alternate evenings, however, we basked in the warmth of the drawing room with its low beamed ceiling and the heat from the log fire seemed to reach every corner of the room.

Memory is a queer thing — one can have a very vivid picture in one's mind but have no recollection of events leading up to it. I can see Dad sat in the armchair by the kitchen range holding his frozen hands in front of the blaze. It is late afternoon in the winter — it must be a Thursday and Dad had driven the horse and trap from Devizes Market in a snowstorm. On the table is a cyclamen — a present for Mother from the flower stall in the Shambles, I imagine. The crimson blossoms are a glowing pool of light on the brown velvet tablecloth and contrasted strangely with the blue veined hands held in front of the bars of the kitchen range.

There always seemed to be a few weeks in the winter when the weather was really cruel, too severe to venture outside for any length of time. Peg and I were then forced to spend days inside.

We had a table on the back landing, which we claimed as our own — it had two drawers in which we kept all our bits and pieces. Exercise books full of scribble, large scrapbooks in which we pasted numerous coloured pictures from seed catalogues in a hotch potch arrangement. We also pressed wild flowers between thin tissue paper, putting them between the pages of the heaviest books we could find. They ended up losing both colour and shape and smelling fusty. From the bathroom, next door to the landing, we filled paste pots from the cold water tap and got out an ancient painting box. As we endeavoured to soften the dried up squares of water paints, the water in the pots became murkier and our colours more diffused.

Perhaps our most cherished possession was a complete set of horse's teeth, which we kept in a matchbox. From the outside there were nothing to distinguish these from an ordinary box of safety matches. At times we would mislay the teeth and the box would find its way down into the kitchen, the family getting quite accustomed to finding it there. However, a visitor wishing to light a candle in the twilight was horrified when her groping fingers touched our "equestrian molars" instead of a match!

Christmas over, a few childrens' parties at local houses brightened up the short January days. The one Peg and I enjoyed most was held yearly at Scott's Farm, Stockley, the home of the Dews. The games they organised were more exciting, and teas more lavish, and the other child guests older and more interesting. In fact some were old enough for silk stockings and grown up clothes. We would lap up every detail and discuss this at length later in the year.

One unforgettable occasion, we arrived on the wrong Saturday for the party. We crunched our way up the gravelled drive in the early twilight of the cold winter afternoon, past the ilex oak and rang the bell on the front door. I don't know why the absence of cars on the drive, or the unlit front windows didn't make us realise what was wrong.

Mrs Dew had a maid, not just a "woman in" but a resident maid, which made them seem quite opulent in our eyes. Elsie, in her afternoon uniform, answered the bell. If one of us had suddenly developed two heads, she couldn't have looked more horror struck. Without a word, she vanished down the hall and we heard the following snippets of conversation.

"The two little Coleses are 'ere, Mam," breathlessly from Elsie.

"Oh dear, how unfortunate! I'd better come and explain." This from Mrs Dew.

It was only then the whole sad situation unfolded before us. Clutching our house shoes, still in their brown paper bag, we made for home.

"By next Saturday," I said to Peg as we rounded the Knap, "One of us could have measles, or broken a leg."

"Might even be dead," Peg added gloomily.

One year there was a Fancy Dress party at the Recreational Hall in Calne. This was quite an innovation on the part of several relations and friends who joined forces and hired the Hall for the occasion, instead of holding individual parties in their own homes. The Fancy Dress idea caused great problems in our own house. I don't think Dick can have been invited or else he had a good excuse not to attend because he didn't seem to figure in the discussion.

Barbara settled for going dressed as "Night". In our eyes she looked ravishing in lots of black muslin, sprinkled with stars and sequins and to cap it all, a half moon, made of silver paper and cardboard, rose majestically from behind one ear. The general idea was for Peg to attend as a fairy — she was a natural for the part, small, blue-eyed with blonde curls. That left me, a stocky six-year-old, without a costume.

I didn't see why I couldn't be a fairy as well and let the family know it quite forcibly. It says quite a lot for the tactfulness of the rest that no one said "Because you're too darned fat". In sympathy Peg said she wasn't too keen on being a fairy either and got unjustly accused of being awkward as well.

In the end Mother, showing one of her brilliant burst of ingenuity in an emergency, produced a long dress and made a poke bonnet and I was persuaded to go as a Victorian lady. The general effect was quite good as

Mother even made a posy of artificial flowers surrounded by a paper doily.

Dad said I looked very nice but would we hurry up and get out so that he could have a little peace and quiet.

I think that on the whole we enjoyed the party. I kept leaving my posy on chairs when I joined in the games, with the result that it frequently got sat upon and the artificial flowers wilted as though they were real ones. Peg as usual stayed immaculate as ever but, towards the end of the evening, Barbara's new moon had slipped somewhat and it now inappropriately resembled a halo.

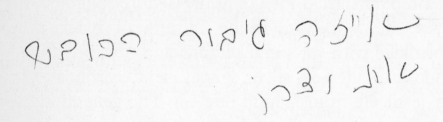

CHAPTER SEVEN

Hey Days and Holidays

The Annual Flower Show was the biggest village event and we enjoyed every moment of it. From the time the cavalcade of painted caravans, carts, trailers etc., passed along the road carrying the roundabouts, side-shows and the rest of the funfair until they had packed up and left the show field, the whole atmosphere was charged with excited anticipation.

I suppose we must have had wet Flower Show days but I can only seem to remember the fine ones. Hazy sunshine in the morning, leading to hot sunny afternoons followed by warm evenings and clear starry nights.

We were all up early on Flower Show day — Mother would have made several entries in the various classes and for days would have been selecting, discarding, re-selecting and finally her ultimate choice would be lined up in the shed. Bright aster heads pushed through cardboard covered with black velvet, their stems in little paste pots, out of sight behind the cardboard. Sweet peas in long thin glass vases, the maidenhair fern in the green china jardiniere looking green and fresh as all its dead fronds had been cut away with nail scissors. Brown eggs on a white doily, white eggs on black velvet and the dish of beautifully floury potatoes, garlanded with sprig of parsley.

Some of the exhibits would be carefully loaded onto the floor of the "tub" whilst we nursed the more fragile, breakable things. Quite often we transported Auntie Edie's exhibits to the show as well as our own. These would invariably include her giant aspidistra, which had won first prize in the "Foliage Plant" section for a succession of years. Its leaves, shiny from a recent sponge down in milk and water, would be carefully lifted into the tub and take up at least a third of the available space. If a slight accident should happen to it *en route*, thought Peg and I, Mother would have stood more chance with her fern. It would not have needed a big accident, just a leaf or two broken off to spoil the symmetry and the "Green Giant" would be defeated. However we would arrive at the show ground with everything intact, including our two jam jars of wild flowers for the children's classes. We would have scoured the countryside to find sufficient variety — there would be all the taller things such as willow herbs, the different sorts of grasses, meadowsweet, ragged robins in the centre, while round the outside would be the smaller vetches etc. From the withy beds in the field bordering the farm, we got the meadowsweet and campions; from the downs the round headed rampions, knapweed etc.

In the large flower show tent it was a hive of activity, with everyone hurrying to finish before the judges arrived at 11.30a.m. Auntie Edie would arrive later by bike, dismounting at the gate and wheeling her "sit up and beg" bicycle with the string dress guards over the bumpy grass to the tent. There was a smell of vegetables and damp grass and the conversation was hushed as in a church. Two churns of water stood outside for the use of the exhibitors and Peg and I amused ourselves by carrying it in cans to the various trestle tables.

Auntie Edie would have finished with her other exhibits and be starting on her table decoration. This was well worth watching. First a cloth was spread over her part of the table and out came her "Epergne" and four little vases, one for each corner of the cloth. Everyone used very dainty flowers for these arrangements, with lots of asparagus fern, and there would be pastel-shaded sweet peas with gysophilas, red carnations with bright blue lobelia trailing from the side vases. One year there was an arrangement of red roses. Peg and I though it was perfect — the centrepiece was silver, or at least of that colour and the deep crimson blooms were reflected in the sides of the vases.

"First prize for sure" we told each other with conviction. No one could have been more surprised than we were, when later we found that our favourite one had a Reserve card. To make matters worse on the bottom of the card was written in thick black ink **"Far too heavy an arrangement"**. The First Prize had gone to pale pink and mauve cosmos, which in our opinion were nowhere near as beautiful as the deep red roses. One year the Miss Knowlers (two spinster ladies from Heddington) had used pink rambler roses placed on a white cloth to make the words "Home Sweet Home". It looked quite nice in the morning, but with the heat of the afternoon, the flowers faded from lack of water and it looked just like a heap of rose prunings.

When we got fed up with the inside of the tent, we sat outside by the entrance, leant up against the thick guy ropes, and watched the people coming and going. Tommy Gartside the roadman would arrive, a large dahlia in his buttonhole, carrying two enormous marrows, his face beaming. Freddie Summers had all his exhibits in a large handcart, which he had trundled all the way from West View Cottages, Stockley. The cart was spilling over with flowers and vegetables and it almost looked as if had a flower show on its own. Auntie Edie left, wheeling her bicycle to the entrance again, secateurs and spare unused flowers in the basket in the front.

At last Mother would have finished, every one by this time under pressure to leave to make way for the judges. Folk would have one last lingering look at their exhibits, casting side-glances at others in the same class and mentally assessing their chances.

On the way to the gate were the caravans — romantic they seemed when the half doors were opened and one glimpsed all the brightness of the brass and glass and colourful fittings. In contrast the fair folk seemed drab — the children silent and watchful, like tiny adults in their long skirts. The women folk were washing their clothes and hanging them over the thick hedge transforming it into a colourful patchwork quilt. At night, behind the hoopla and the coconut shies, these women would seem different, younger, more glamorous with flashing earrings and gaudy beads accentuated by the flickering naphtha lights. With smiling faces they would laugh and joke with the crowd and with one another but for now they seemed sullen and ill humoured.

One year when we reached the gate of the Flower Show field a young gypsy lad was being escorted to the road, flanked on either side by a policeman. The other caravan dwellers stood by silently in a little group. At the door of one of the vans stood an old gypsy woman. Her cheeks resembled a walnut shell, wrinkled and brown and down these furrows tears ran their uneven course. We never did discover just what crime that young boy had committed but for a while the fear in his eyes made us unhappy until all the pleasures of the afternoon put it out of our minds.

It would seem ages from the time we reached home in the morning until we could go back to the show when it opened at 2.30p.m. The sports were at 3.00p.m., but we always planned to walk around the flower tent and view the prize cards beforehand. There would be many doing the same thing — some happy with the results, beaming as they stood near the entrance, ready for the congratulations. Others were not so pleased with the results or the judging.

"They taters ben't worth a fust, be 'un," someone grumbled.

"If they do say h'annuals, they do mean h'annuals not b. . . p'renuls" from another.

The sports started at 3.00p.m., and Peg and I relied on the prize money from these to finance the rest of the day. Any money due from winning with the wild flowers was rather a dead loss, as we would not receive that until a week or so after the show. Prize money for the sports, however, one got at the finishing tape which was a very satisfactory arrangement; two shillings for a First Place, one shilling and sixpence for a Second Place and one shilling for Third, and I believe there was a Fourth prize of sixpence.

Peg and I were fairly sure of the first prize for the three-legged race; we would have been practising hard for at least a fortnight beforehand. We would have chased up and down the road with one of Dad's handkerchiefs tied firmly round our legs until we became most proficient at it. We could even leap over fallen competitors lying on the ground without losing our rhythm. Peg would also win the fifty yards sprint, with luck I might manage a third or fourth but there could be several girls faster than me. However we always shared our prize money right down the middle. Who would win the egg and spoon race was anybody's guess. To start with the eggs, china ones gathered I imagine from the local farms, were all different sizes, as were the spoons. If one was fortunate enough to get both a large, top-heavy egg plus a small spoon, one's chances were virtually nil. There were also those who held their egg down with their thumb — they might be noticed and sent back to start again but if not they would go on to an unlawful win. Between us we generally managed to win enough money for the day and Dick and Barbara, who ran like hares, did likewise in the older children's races.

Later on there were the adults' sports; the motor cycling races were the most exciting. The competitors roared into the ring on their old James, Matchless, or Douglas machines, revved up and away, smoke billowing from the exhaust. There would also be a tug-of-war and one year a pillow fight on a greasy pole.

A free tea was arranged for the children at 5.00p.m. It took place in the Mission Room, a red brick building at the other end of the Common. If fine, and it always seemed to be, the tea was brought outside to the row of children sat on forms in the sunshine. Slab cake, seed cake and plates of bread and butter were handed round. All this was very pleasant but as we didn't want to miss too much of the Show we didn't linger there and we were soon once more running down the long track to the Show Field.

The men's sport always ended with the Marathon race. At least it was called by that name although the competitors actually ran the distance round the roads of Stockley and Heddington, starting and finishing with the Show Field. By the time the First prizewinners arrived and breathlessly staggered the last few yards into the field, dusk would be falling. Others arrived spasmodically and some that had fallen by the wayside hitched a lift on the pillion of the adjudicators' bikes. These adjudicators placed themselves at intervals along the route to prevent the participants from taking a short cut across the fields. Vic Lewis, from Bromham, would be sure to be the winner, in fact he would win most of the men's prizes, and had done so for years. Born in a different age and in different circumstances he would probably have made an Olympic competitor.

The end of the sports meant that we could devote all our time and interest to the funfair. Bromham Brass Band who had been playing non-stop had finished all their stirring marches and the members had repaired to the Beer Tent and the music from the Fairground Organ took over. The brightly coloured carved figures on the front moved jerkily and not quite in time with the music.

The roundabouts were the favourite of ours. They had quite a slack time whilst folk were watching the sports but now there would be a queue waiting for the horses to slow down and stop. One got an entirely fresh view of the field from the back of one of the horses. Climbing high towards the colourful canopy, a shuddering jerk when one felt that the wooden charger was going to break away from the golden plated rod and then plunge back down towards the revolving dais. When one was high in the air, the stalls took on a different aspect. Looking down on the sweet stall, there seemed to be a sea of candyfloss with mounds of brown and cream barley sugar, forming little islands. On the other side the celluloid windmills on sticks and the balloons on strings formed an ever-changing kaleidoscope of colours. The swinging boats were doing a roaring trade now, in the afternoon they had been occupied by young children being gently swung to and fro by parents or by the man in charge but now they had a different clientele. Youths and girls swung higher and higher until it looked as if they would go over the top, some of the braver ones standing up in the boats to get more leverage on the ropes.

The field seemed full of people now. Mothers trundled their deep prams with the small wheels that were fashionable in those days, their tiny occupants peering over the high sides. Older brothers or sisters drooped on their father's shoulders, fighting the sleep that threatened to overcome them. Beyond the circle of lights and colours were the grey fields, their hedges black in the night, and shadowy cattle stood by the dividing gate, motionless in the darkness, puzzled by this intrusion on their solitude. Everywhere there was laughter, deep-throated guffaws from the Beer Tent, and shrill bursts of excited mirth from the funfair.

Eventually Mother gathered up her brood and we made for home across the common and down the hill past Prince Brown's Farm (his real name was Albert Edward Brown — hence the nickname).

Before we went to sleep, we leant out of our bedroom window and we would still hear, faintly in the distance, the noise of the fair and there would be a slight golden glow in the sky from the lights. It seemed an awfully long time until next August and the next Flower Show.

As the show was the high spot of the summer, so Christmas would be the most eagerly anticipated part of the winter.

The Christmas preparations were spread over a longer period. We started preparing sometime beforehand, beginning with the making of the decorations. We cut wallpaper into strips and, by means of a messy flour and water paste, strung them all together to make a chain. These we hung across the low kitchen ceiling, which meant that everyone over about five foot in height got hopelessly entangled in them.

The Bowood Estate would send to each tenant farmer a brace of pheasants and a large bunch of holly. This would arrive about a week before Christmas and the holly would be cut into pieces by Mother and we would stick a piece behind each picture on the wall.

In spite of good resolutions, Mother rarely got our Christmas puddings done by "stir-up" Sunday. Like all children we enjoyed the making of these, the preparing of the fruit, everything needing to be either cleaned or stoned. Our favourite task was to cut up the thick curved pieces of candied peel into thin strips — I suspect this was in order to have first claim to the coveted pieces of crystallised sugar lining the peel. The high spot of the pudding making was, of course, the addition of several bottles of stout which Dad would have bought from the Ivy Pub the previous night. The dark potent smelling liquid was poured on and then we had a stir. It needed quite a lot of effort to rotate the wooden spoon in the thick glutinous mixture which smelt of spices and fruit. Peg and I would pour the dregs from the stout bottles into tumblers of water and pretend that the weak tea coloured liquid was strong liquor.

Mother and Dad would be working flat out during the last few days before Christmas getting poultry ready for various Christmas orders. Dick and Barbara were old enough to help and even Peg and I were called in to pull the stubby feathers from the last few cockerels and turkeys. It always seemed a cold, depressing job and such a worry being responsible for everyone else's Christmas dinner.

One of Mother's customers for poultry at Christmas was a Russian Countess, who lived in an old gamekeeper's cottage behind Whetham House. Dick and Barbara would normally deliver her bird on their bikes and would tell us all about it when they came back. The Countess apparently escaped from Russia after the Revolution and Peg and I thought her a most romantic sort of person. She must have been quite a recluse, not setting foot outside the Whetham Estate so Dick and Barbara were the only ones who really knew her at all.

The village handbell ringers would call sometimes during Christmas week. We were about the last visit on their list so normally we would have gone to bed before their arrival. They would have been entertained with refreshment at a number of houses besides quite a lengthy stay at the Ivy Pub. By the time they gathered outside our front porch they were fairly inebriated and their timing was somewhat erratic as they "ding donged" their way through some of the well-known carols.

Mother would hide all the presents as they came by post, but Barbara would generally manage to find them and by a little detective work of squeezing and poking, would have a fairly good idea what each parcel contained and who it was from. She would then report back to the rest of us. One Christmas she found the pile of presents on the top shelf of the large airing cupboard in the end bedroom and made her examination. Christmas Day arrived and the workbasket from Auntie Bessie was not amongst her pile of presents. She was in a quandary and asked the advice of the rest of us. We all came to the same conclusion — there was nothing she could do without Mother knowing about her finding the presents. At Easter, during the annual spring clean, the missing present came to light. It had fallen down behind the large hot water tank and Barbara got her belated gift. I don't think it taught her a lesson, she still made an extensive search for the family's presents each year!

Auntie Dora would normally come to spend a few days over the holiday and this would make everything that much more enjoyable. On Christmas Eve all the poultry would be finished and delivered and the whole family could relax. It was then that we could begin to think that Christmas was finally here.

We always longed for snow but it would arrive before Christmas Day and be gone or else it would wait for the New Year. Whatever the weather we normally took quite a long walk on Christmas afternoon. Sometimes we would go to the top of Stockley Hollow and walk across to the hunting gate, looking from there to Kings Play which would seem cold and distant, shrouded in mist. Another year we might go down to Broad's Green until we reached the Long Road leading into Calne. The pale winter sunshine would lighten the sombre mass of fir trees in the copse by the brook. By the time we got home it would be dusk and we'd feel warm, hungry and ready for our tea.

Barbara took pride in preparing the tea table. She would do quite an elaborate table centre using a mirror decorated with imitation snow, red ribbons and holly. One year she made a snowman of cotton wool. Hanging from its waist were labelled strings — one for each member of the family, the idea being that at a given signal each person would pull his or her respective string and release the present. Something went wrong, however, and the little gifts got hopelessly tangled up inside the snowman and the whole thing had to be taken apart to release them.

CHAPTER
EIGHT

Relatives

Mother had two sisters and one surviving brother — a younger brother having died soon after the Great War leaving a widow and two baby daughters. Auntie Dora was, of course, the sister that we knew the best because she so often stayed with us for quite long periods. However, we saw quite a lot of Auntie Win who lived at Beversbrook, a farm on the Hilmarton Road from Calne.

She and Uncle Will had a big house and a large family of seven children. Life at Beversbrook seemed to be perfect, the garden weed free and productive, the tennis court immaculate and in the large cool rooms the furniture gleamed from constant polishing. The teas were good too, sponge cakes had risen high and light and the butter icing was thick and delicious. There were fruit cakes with more cherries than we were accustomed to and scones that melted in the mouth.

Auntie Win had one of those laughing faces — sometimes her large family must caused her worry and anxiety but it never showed in her smiling face. Uncle Will was plump and merry. He was justly proud of his garden. The vegetable garden was enclosed in a high brick wall and seemed to stretch for miles. Here there were greenhouse and frames full of plants and fruit trees clambered up the high-bricked walls to fruit well in such a sunny sheltered situation.

In front of the house was a conservatory and here grew a vine which bore large black juicy grapes. This vine must have been a great age because Uncle Will's father had planted it years ago, on top of the grave of his favourite black horse! Uncle Will always told us this tale as he was selecting one of the best bunches for us to sample. Peg and I wished he didn't — the inference was that the black hunter had been a constant source of manure over the decades!

At Beversbrook there always seemed to be young people around, even with half the children away at school or following their own pursuits, there always seemed enough left to play croquet. The mallets and balls were kept in a large oak chest in the hall and there were mallets to suit all tastes and all ages, so different from our own limited supply where someone always had to have the one with the cracked handle. We played on the long lawn in front of the house where the formal flower beds edged with little short box hedges gave the whole garden an Elizabethan appearance. There was a yucca tree in a bed by the drive, prickly and uninteresting most of the time but a thing of beauty when it flowered.

When we got tired of croquet, there was always hide and seek in the rick-yard. Here there was a large granary perched high on saddle stones and the sleek brown hens scratched around in the loose straw from between the neatly thatched hayricks.

Uncle Percy, Mother's only surviving brother, lived at Church Farm, Seagry, the farm where Mother and her brothers and sisters were brought up. We didn't visit here very frequently as Seagry was some distance from Stockley, far further than the journey to Beversbrook.

There was a very fine stone archway spanning the drive before one reached the farm; this I think is now the property of the National Trust. Leading from the pathway through the churchyard to the little village church was the family graves. Mother would visit them and tell us about the Godwins and Teagles named on the tall grey tombstones. Great-Grandfather Godwin who was the miller at the Old Mill House and whose son came to live at Church Farm and the Great-Aunts from the Close — Aunt Phyllis and Aunt Sophia. Aunt Sophia had left the leafy lane of Seagry to do social work in the East End of London. To us she seemed a very heroic figure. To exchange her secure, happy life at the Close for the dirt and disease of the slums seemed a most noble thing to do.

Peg and I had never known either of our Grandparents or for that matter any Great-Aunts or Uncles. This always seemed a sad deprivation — other children's older relatives always seemed indulgent and inclined to spoil their small kin. We seemed to miss out on all this.

Uncle Percy and Auntie Lil had three daughters, older than Peg and me, more the age group of Dick and Barbara. All three were keen horse riders and very good at it. The four of us had no inclination to ride, just as well as there would never have been sufficient money to buy the necessary gear. Barbara put this lack of equestrian enthusiasm down to the fact that all the horses at the farm were slightly neurotic.

"Riding behind them in a pony trap was nerve racking enough," she said, "Without actually mounting their backs!"

They were certainly anything but bomb proof, the slightest noise or a fleeting glance at anything unfamiliar was enough to start them bucking and rearing. One summer afternoon we were parked outside Lloyd's Bank in Calne whilst Mother and Dad had a lengthy discussion with the Bank Manager, probably about the overdraft! Barbara was in the pony trap with Peg and me and between the shafts was Ginger — an ex-polo pony with an excitable nature. For some unknown reason Ginger started to back onto the pavement. Like a rat leaving a sinking ship Barbara leapt over the side of the trap to the safety of the road. I believe that passers-by rescued Peg and me whilst Barbara was hunting for our parents in the Bank.

We loved Mother to tell us about her childhood at Seagry. She showed us the wall where the gleanies used to gather on Sunday nights and their cries of "Go back! Go back!" would interrupt the sermon during Evensong, much to the embarrassment of the Godwin family. In fact in the end one of the household would stay behind from church and shoo the offending gleanies away from the wall to a suitable distance where their irreverent interruptions could not be heard by the congregation. It seemed that gleanies would be quite a source of worry to Mother throughout her life. We also liked Mother's tale of the late visitor at the farm who, having taken a short cut home through the churchyard to the village, was terrified by a ghostly apparition which appeared to be rising from one of the graves. Later on it was found to be nothing more sinister than a white donkey which had strayed from a nearby farm.

The children of Mother's younger brother, Uncle Edgar, who died shortly after the Great War, were also girls. This meant that in our own particular branch of the family the Godwin name would die out.

We liked Auntie Beattie, the young widow of Uncle Edgar. She had soft brown eyes in a dimpled face and a mop of dark brown hair which always seemed to be escaping from her hairpins. She also had a deep voice with a chuckle built into it. Modern for that day and age, she drove a small car and coped most successfully in bringing up her family on her own.

To say we had no Great-Aunts is not strictly correct. Great-Aunt Emma lived at Bloomfield Avenue, Bath, and Mother, orphaned at an early age, had made her home there until her marriage. We often wondered how our country-loving mother with her fondness for the fields, animals and flowers could have been really happy in a city. It was on a visit to Auntie Edie, then at Lower Farm, Heddington, that she met and eventually married Dad. Great-Aunt Emma's eldest daughter had married a Baronet, which put her on a different sort of level from the rest of the relatives.

"Whatever would Aunt Emma say?" Mother would exclaim when life became extra chaotic at the farm.

Once a year Mother made a pilgrimage to the house in Bloomfield Avenue for Aunt Emma's annual inspection of her children. We didn't really enjoy the train journey as most of the way from Chippenham to Green Park Station, Bath, Mother was entreating us to behave well and, above all, not to talk too much. This warning might have been necessary in the case of Dick and Barbara but as far as Peg and I were concerned we were overawed to the extent of being speechless! From the moment Mary, the rather grim faced maid, opened the imposing front door to us to the time we thankfully trotted down the steps to the pavement we barely said a word.

Great-Aunt Emma's house was a perfect example of Edwardian elegance. Peg and I sat on the red velvet chaise longue, afraid to lean back too far in case we creased the wrinkle free antimacassar and scared of leaning too far forwards in case we pitched head first into the deep pile grey carpet. Tea brought its problems as well — we were not used to balancing our cups of tea while trying to eat wafer-thin sandwiches.

However, the visit over, our natural exuberance soon returned and we enjoyed the brightly lit shops, the crowded pavements and the train journey home.

Uncle Frank and Auntie Bessie lived at Manor Farm, Little Somerford. I believe Auntie Bessie was a cousin of Mother's, so that would have made her a second cousin to us.

Uncle Frank was jovial, handsome with a bristling moustache. We didn't much like being kissed by him because of this moustache but he was very generous with half crowns. Unfortunately he had the habit of tipping them down the back of our clothes! If one was lucky they dropped straight through, but if not they got horribly tangled up with liberty bodices and knickers and caused Peg and me great embarrassment. On the whole it was worth it — two and sixpence being quite a sum in those days, the spending of which would take a lot of pleasant planning.

Auntie Bessie was plump and nearly blind. They were a childless couple and apparently, along with the family doctor, had been quite willing to adopt me at birth. I often thought of this other life I could be leading — parted from Peg and doomed to a life of bristling kisses. Even the thought of boundless half crowns would not have compensated for that.

Auntie Dora made her home with Auntie Bessie, so when we were about five years old Peg and I went to Manor Farm for a week's holiday.

The main thing that interested us about the Farm was the beautiful old twisted Monkey Puzzle tree on the smooth lawn. We had never seen one before. The stable clock in the sunlit yard came a close second.

We would spend long hours in the kitchen with the two maids, Gertrude and Edith, who were sisters. Gertrude was large and big boned and did quite a lot of the housework whilst Edith was small and rosy and helped at table. They were both bad travellers in bus, car or train. Flying being still in its infancy, I don't suppose they had tried that! The result of this was that they cycled everywhere, which must have taken up quite a lot of their days off.

"Could only just have got there when it was time to come away again," said Peg.

Auntie Bessie still liked a game of croquet although she found it difficult because of her bad sight. Auntie Dora would tie a white handkerchief on the top of the hoop Auntie Bessie was aiming at. While the grownups were playing, Peg and I sat in the thatched summerhouse, which was inclined to be earwiggy but nice and private. Here we could discuss in private all the details of the visit. One of the things that intrigued us most was the fact that Uncle Frank had a dressing room. We couldn't for the life of us see why he couldn't have undressed in front of Auntie Bessie, who in any case couldn't see very well! It was a wonder we didn't approach Uncle Frank about this, or at least Auntie Dora, but I don't think we did either.

Life at Manor Farm was so unlike life at Stockley Farm. Uncle Frank let us beat the brass gong in the hall and we sat down to elegant meals, laid out in style in the dining room — very different from our own kitchen table.

While we were there we went to Cirencester Park to see a polo match. We didn't enjoy it very much as we felt sorry for the horses — they just get into a good gallop towards one goal, only to be pulled up quickly and forced to go in quite a different direction. There were compensations in the shape of a picnic lunch in a hamper in the back of the car. The hamper was beautifully fitted out with all sorts of cutlery and china slotted into the wickerwork and with containers of lovely sandwiches and salads.

Uncle Arthur was the oldest of Dad's brothers. He lived at Keynsham and had a factory at Bristol which made "Blood and Bone" fertiliser. Profitable, I suppose, but smelly — in later years whenever we approached Temple Mead Station by train, we always imagined we could smell the factory which gave us a mixed feeling of pride and embarrassment.

Uncle Arthur had many interests and we were never quite sure which was the current one as they changed so often.

One October afternoon he and Auntie Katie came to tea and Uncle Arthur was laden down with textbooks on "*Edible Fungi*", the collecting of toadstools having apparently replaced playing the pianola which was his last interest!

I think it must have been Dick who mentioned that he knew where there was a beef steak fungi growing on one of the old oaks in the Common Field. Apparently "*Fistuline hepatica*" was just what Uncle Arthur wanted so, although it was nearly teatime, we set off to get it.

It was a long journey to the Common Field — Dick led the way, closely followed by Uncle Arthur and Barbara while Peg and I brought up the rear. By the time we reached the trees it was getting quite late. Uncle Arthur hacked away at the revolting looking spongy material while a mist came over the fields and it grew chilly. We thought of tea laid out at home and

Mother and Auntie Katie sitting chatting by a bright fire and wished he would hurry up.

Finally he had gathered sufficient spoils and we made for home — Uncle Arthur in the lead this time, his bald head shining in the gathering dusk. I don't know how long this latest craze lasted but I think it had been replaced by something new the next time he visited us.

Auntie Katie would send Mother parcels of clothes outgrown by her own family. These must have been more useful to us as they were always of such good quality that no amount of tree climbing or rough usage seemed to spoil them. Sometimes we longed for something brand new, cheap and cheerful. Barbara, especially, was of an age when she was just beginning to be clothes conscious. I don't think that it worried Peg and me greatly. Providing we were allowed to be barelegged in the summer and had sufficient warm clothes to keep out the cold in the winter, we were happy.

We rebelled occasionally about always being dressed alike — Mother thought it appropriate for twins although we really didn't resemble each other at all. Of course the system fell down when one of two identical dresses was torn, grubby or buttonless. This generally happened to mine without any noticeable effort on my part, so we were quite often dressed differently through necessity.

We once had a phase when we passionately wanted to do away with fringes and have a side parting in our hair. Miss Clifton had given us some magazines and we were very taken with one of the illustrations therein. We borrowed two of Dad's tiepins and scraped back our short front bits of hair from crooked partings. The tiepins kept slipping out and the results didn't look a bit like the model in the glossy magazine so, much to Mother's relief, we reverted to our fringes once more.

Another of Dad's brothers had a draper's shop in Calne. According to Dad, Uncle Walter, because of his unfortunate initials "W.C." had been known as "Privy" at boarding school. To us this seemed quite incongruous as Uncle Walter seemed far too dignified for such levity.

We liked going to J. H. Cole and Sons, Drapers and Outfitters. The shopwalker, Mr Gabb, would produce a cane chair for Mum and summon one of the assistants from the rear of the shop. We wondered if Mum got special treatment because she was a relative. Sometimes it all seemed rather a lot of fuss for two yards of knicker elastic.

Quite by chance we discovered that the female shop assistants had a most unusual lavatory. It was I who went there the first time, accompanied by one of the assistants whilst Mother made her purchase. I had never seen one like it — there was a flight of steps and on the pinnacle stood the toilet. I could hardly wait to tell Peg all about it. From then on, when Mother was shopping, one of us would express a desire to spend a penny and the other would go along for company or "just in case".

I would sit regally on the top, while Peg like some lowly courtier, crouched at the bottom. We would then reverse the roles until there was grim danger of Mother banging on the door, fearing that we had some major tummy upset. I imagine the staff must have thought there was something drastically wrong with our bladders. Mother would give us a little lecture on the bad timing of our calls to Nature. We would dearly have loved a lavatory like that at home. We wondered if the plump smiling lady from the bedding department or the small dark girl from the haberdashery in the lower shop realised their good fortune. How nice to be on the staff and visit there at will, we thought.

Auntie Kit was Uncle Walter's wife and our Godmother. We were often asked back to their home at the back of the shop — it was in these large heavily furnished rooms that Dad, his brothers and one sister had grown up when Grandfather Cole ran the shop. There was a large garden, secluded lawns and shrubs, now alas, all torn down to make way for road improvements and housing.

Jack and Marjorie Cole was older than we were and we saw them infrequently. They spent a long time in London — Jack learning about the drapery trade and Marjorie training to be a nurse. When we did catch sight of them, they were on holiday, running through the shop carrying tennis racquets, looking grown up and unapproachable.

CHAPTER
NINE

Our Animals

The first pet dog I can remember at the farm was Bruce, the spaniel. I believe he figured more in Dick's and Barbara's childhood, as he was quite elderly when Peg and I were small. He died soon after. The next dog, Jock, a black retriever, played a large part in our lives. He loved all children intensely, but hated other dogs and would fight fiercely all canine intruders without being in the least provoked by them. His passion for children extended beyond the family circle and if a pram was being pushed along the road he would walk alongside, his black head thrust under the hood, while he tried to give the young occupant a lick or so. This would cause quite a lot of consternation on the part of the pram pusher, especially if not particularly fond of dogs.

He found quite a lot of admiration at the row of cottages near the farm, where there was a number of young children. They would all line up for Jock to push them down with his big paws, then get up again for the process to be repeated.

Then there was the dreadful day when he was knocked down and mortally injured by a passing car.

So few cars would pass along our road that it seemed to us all so unfair that he should have been on the road just at the wrong moment. We missed him and mourned for him terribly and even when Dad brought home the small bundle of fur which was Chum, the border collie, we still remembered Jock and felt guilty at loving this newcomer.

Chum was so different from Jock, highly-strung and temperamental. He only loved the family and before he had barely got through the puppy stage he was the scourge of the neighbourhood. He lived to a tremendous age, having had far more than his allotted nips at folk. However, he adored the family and his devotion to them, I believe, led to his saving Peg from being attacked by a frenzied cow. This story does not rightly belong to the decade of my book but the telling of it might vindicate Chum from some of his other sins.

Peg was collecting eggs and feeding the hens in a field some distance from the farm, unaware that a cow, normally placid but vicious immediately after calving, was in one corner of the field with her newborn calf. Seeing Peg walking with the bucket of food and her basket towards the henhouse, the cow charged at her. Chum must have summed up the situation in a flash because he made for the corner and barked furiously at the small calf, thereby causing a diversion. The cow turned and chased after Chum, leaving Peg to spring across to the gate and safety.

We had numerous cats at the farm and normally we allotted one to each member of the family. Some were more outstanding in character than others and these have lived in my memory to this day.

Barbara's favourite cat was a small tabby called Punch, a neat clean little thing with a reasoning mind. Knowing that the majority of newborn kittens would generally be disposed of, she would go to great lengths to keep her litters hidden until their eyes were open. The ideal place was in the warmth and the darkness of the hayloft above the stables. When they were several weeks old, she would carry them by the scruff of their fat little necks, one by one, down the steps. With head held high, she would walk with her fluffy offsprings to the kitchen door, knowing full well that at their age they would have to be kept and homes found for them.

My own particular pet, a black tom called Samuel Sebastian, was quite useless either as a ratter or a mouser. When hungry, I think he would condescend to catch the occasional young rabbit and would arrive home with his battered ears outlined with rabbit fleas. He would also disappear for days on courting expeditions, and I would mourn for him until suddenly he reappeared, a few more battle scars on his thin face and perhaps another piece missing from his ears. There was nothing attractive about his rusty lean black body but I loved him very much.

We kept three of his offspring. Punch, the mother, had found another successful hiding place for this particular litter. Mother called two of them Joel and Abiah, but as the biblical Samuel only had two sons she called the third one X. X would sit on the blackleaded trivet in front of the bars of the range and the heat from the red coals would eventually singe the fur on one side of his body. The smell of burned fur would permeate the kitchen. "X is on fire again!" someone would shout and rush to extinguish him. He never learnt his lesson and within a very short time he was back in his usual hot seat.

For a short while Peg and I had a very pretty little kitten called Podge. He had a black pencil of a tail and a deep-throated purr which rocked his little fat body. Unfortunately Podge's habit of catching and eating baby birds spread to our own livestock, nothing was safe from his sharp claws and needle teeth. Turkey poults, baby chicks and gleanies, all suffered the same fate. The family did all they could to break him of this habit but he still persisted in this barbarism until, in the end, he had to be put down. Peg and I were heartbroken and inconsolable for several days, unfairly blaming everyone and insisting that we would not have left Podge out of our sight if he had been allowed to live. We seemed to spend quite a lot of time grieving over pets, although on the whole we must have got more pleasure than pain from them.

Of all the creatures on the farm, I would imagine General, the big white carthorse, had the most character. General had been to war and in the mud and horror of France had used his great strength to pull a gun carrier. Shipped back to Blighty, shell-shocked and blind in one eye, he had been put up for sale in a local horse auction for ex war-horses and there had the great good fortune to be brought by Dad. I don't think there were many bidders for the General, who had the reputation for being savage. Now Dad understood and loved horses and from then on the old warrior was in good hands. General was quite placid until it thundered or he heard a gun shot, then the poor thing thought he was once more back at the front and he'd bolt across fields or over hedges, taking whatever implements he happened to be hitched to with him. Whenever the clouds gathered and the sultry air foretold a thunderstorm, Dad would walk General up and down and talk to him until he became calm.

Sometimes he was used to draw the large trap. I think Dad was always at the reins then, just in case of trouble. On one occasion we were going to Beversbrook, with all the family aboard the trap. Rain started as we neared Calne and an unsuspecting pedestrian raised her umbrella as General trotted up Quemerford, I suppose he must have caught a glimpse of this out of the corner of his good eye and he bolted. Down London Road, New Road and across the Strand he galloped, Dad stood up in his seat and clutched the reins and all of us cowered in our seats. The steep incline of High Street lowered the pace somewhat but we didn't come to a halt until we were on the Hilmarton Road.

After many years of hard work, General was retired and supposed to spend the rest of his days leading a life of leisure, cropping the short grass in the Home Field. Years later, however, the elevator got stuck in the gateway between the Long Ground and More Mead. It had been a very wet summer and this was the last straw. Bonny and Trooper couldn't shift the heavy machinery and it was imperative the rick should be started before the next deluge. "Old General would move it," said Dad. In spite of family opposition the old horse was led out and harnessed to the elevator and, in spite of his age, he pulled the heavy implement clear with ease. He died just before the last war. No-one was quite sure how old he was, but he certainly had an adventurous life.

Not all the creatures on the farm were loveable, however. Take Sammy Sims, a name we bestowed on a vicious leghorn cockerel. He hated all the human race and would make unprovoked attacks on anyone in his path. To make matters worse, he was a roamer and, not content with pecking the legs of the family, would stray onto the road and outlying field to find fresh victims. Poor Annie Summers, peacefully wooding in old Pond Field, would be forced to make for home when Sammy appeared, with her old Army cape flapping round her legs and her ancient pram only half filled with dead wood.

Eventually Sammy was confined to a large grass run and we were warned not to open the wire door and let him out. It was a hot thundery afternoon when Peg and I saw the old saucepan in the corner of the run — it was just what we wanted for the game we were playing. As the afternoon wore on it became more and more important that we retrieved the saucepan. Finally Peg made her plans. I was to go in and get it whilst she caused a diversion outside and then, my mission completed, she would let me out by the wire door. Somehow her plans went wildly astray. Sammy refused to be diverted by Peg hopping up and down and pushing sticks through the wire netting. One couldn't blame him, as I was a much easier target for his beak. Round and round the pen I dashed with Sammy in hot pursuit, pecking at my bare legs.

"Let me out!" I screeched every time I passed the wire door.

"Can't, I shall let Sammy out!" called back Peg, her anxious little face pressed against the wire. Finally I made my escape but not without some bloodshed and we still had not got the saucepan.

A far more formidable looking creature was Rastus, the boar. He did indeed look fierce, with his tusks and slobbering mouth. Actually he rather liked people and would make a dash for folk in the hope that they would scratch him behind his hoary old ears. As a consequence of this he was always let loose in the orchard when the apples were ripe to forestall would be "scrumpers". This wasn't successful as it sounded because Rastus too liked apples and would shake the lower branches of the Tom Putts and Russets and then chomp his way through several pounds of the best eaters.

TAILPIECE

The summer of 1929 was one of the warmest on record, followed by torrential thunderstorms. The Conservative Government had been toppled by the Labour Party and England had her first test match with New Zealand. The papers were full of a young woman aviator, Amy Johnson, but she had yet to make the front pages with her flight to Australia. The R101 was also to make the headlines, no-one foreseeing her tragic end in a year's time.

None of these things seemed of paramount importance to Peg and me. We sat on the cowyard wall on an afternoon in early September, it was warm in the sun, and a clump of elm trees by the gate threw a giant shadow across the grass verge onto the road. Next week at the age of nine and a half, we would start school for the first time. The prospect filled us with excitement, tinged with a little apprehension.

"It's going to be very different." Peg said.

Robato

PART TWO

Potato

CHAPTER ONE

The Prep and Miss Bean

Although Peg and I were, by this time, fairly proficient at riding our bikes, the family decided that, for the time being, we were too inexperienced to ride through Calne to the Grammar School on the Green. Consequently Mother made arrangements for us to leave our bikes at the blacksmith's shop at Quemerford in the morning and collect them again after school. This must have made quite a complicated procedure for the three miles journey. Having safely negotiated Ebor Cottage Corner, I imagine we might have come to no harm for the rest of the journey but, according to Mother, the White Hart Corner was dangerous to anyone on two wheels, even in those days when the horse-drawn traffic probably out-numbered the petrol driven traffic.

Throughout our school days the nearest we got to an accident was when I rode into the back of a stationary laundry van. This all came about because I was having a heated argument with Peg at the time and not concentrating on the road ahead. The van driver was delivering one of his baskets to a house in London

Road and the tailboard was down. My front wheel slid neatly underneath and my bike came to a halt with me upright and still in the saddle. He was understandably rather annoyed as he had to prise me and my bike away from his van!

Leaving our bikes at the blacksmith's did have its advantages as the forge was rather a fascinating place to two nine-year olds. There was the glow of the fire in the murky gloom, where sparks leapt and danced in the darkness and the asthmatic wheezing which issued from the ancient bellows. Then there was the acrid smell from the black aprons the Cleverly brothers wore at their work. Often there was a carthorse tethered in the lane outside — head buried in a nosebag, noisily blowing and snuffling.

We left our bikes at Quemerford for over a year. I can visualise that forge in the early dusk of a December day, when blasts of hot air came from the wide-open doorway to mingle with the icy air outside. In the summer, it was a different scene — the forge became a blazing inferno — smoke-blackened sweat rolled from the reddened eyes of the blacksmith while the water hissed as it came in contact with the red hot metal.

As the weeks went by, we always seemed to have to hurry the last mile to school. Maybe we spent too long at the blacksmith's or maybe we didn't leave in time. It was quite a distance from the bottom of Quemerford to the Green. We hurried through the long shady avenue of trees in Wessington Avenue, where the Trinity School children hung like noisy limpets on the iron railings. When the bell rang they would rush up the long playground through the school's open door at the end, their cries receding in the distance. When we reached the high pavement, we were almost doing a jog trot, only the fear of meeting one or more of the teachers who lodged in the sedate precincts of Shelburne Road made us keep to a fast walk. Rounding the notorious White Hart Corner, we would heave a sigh of relief to see that the Elementary School children were still playing on the Green. It was not 9.00a.m. and we were not late.

But I digress — that first morning we were not late as we made our way a little apprehensively along the high pavements. It was a hot September day but, as it was the start of the Autumn term, we were dressed in the winter uniform. Our legs were unaccustomed to the black woollen stockings, which were sticky in the heat and refused to stay wrinkle-free in spite of tight "circulation restricting" garters just above our knees. Our new gymslips, made to allow for growth, flapped against our calves. We were very conscious of the bright newness of our cap badges in comparison with those of older pupils, which had mellowed beautifully with age and wear.

The Preparatory form at the Grammar School was in sole charge of Miss Constance Bean, who was Froebel trained. This fact seemed to impress Mother when she heard about it. I can remember being rather surprised, on first seeing Miss Bean, that there wasn't some outward sign of this qualification, not exactly "Froebel trained" emblazoned on her forehead, but just something to distinguish her from the ordinary rank and file. However she looked just like a plump kindly farmer's wife. This she was to become in a few years' time, when she married an Evesham farmer and forsook teaching for the Pershore Orchards of Worcestershire.

The school was divided into two separate buildings. The "Prep" form and the Second class, along with the woodwork room, Domestic Science and dining room, were in the old part. On the other side of the Green was the main school with its cluster of classrooms around the Hall and the two playgrounds.

The old part of the school, which housed Miss Bean's charges, was a bleak old building. The ground floor corridor led to a flight of wide stone stairs with an iron balustrade. On the first landing was a group of life sized statues, apparently of Greek gods, as they wore wreaths around their heads and practically nothing else! On the top landing a short corridor to the right led to the Second form room, whilst Miss Bean's pupils were in the room to the left. Here the ceilings were remarkably low in contrast to the rest of the building and the windows were almost at floor level. It always seemed a little too warm, especially in the winter, when the windows were shut and the large "Tortoise" stove was lit.

What appealed to Peg and me most in the Preparatory form were the extra curriculum activities. Our lessons with Mother had been very functional: reading, writing, arithmetic with a little history and geography thrown in for good measure. Then our recreation seemed totally divorced from "lessons".

Now we were introduced to handiwork — we twisted brightly coloured raffia into plaits and wound them into tablemats. We modelled with plasticine and cut shapes out of cardboard which we then coloured with thick waxy crayons. We made bookmarks and kettle-holders and, that first Christmas after our first term, had enough self-made presents to supply all the family and relatives. It was all quite new and exciting.

Miss Bean was very enthusiastic about nature walks and, weather permitting, we would search the fields leading to "The Sands" for rare wild flowers. Another favourite hunting ground were the large fields belonging to Coleman's Farm. Sometimes we took along jam jars in which to put specimens of pond life. Trailing back to school with our trophies, we would line the window sills of the classroom with jars of ladies bedstraw, purple loosestrife, etc. Eventually the flowers faded and the water containing the tadpoles became green and smelly the windowsill was then cleared until the next foray into the countryside. Peg and I were quite good at nature study — we had, of course, had every opportunity to spend more time out of doors than most of the other pupils, because of our delayed schooling.

Miss Bean held a dancing class for her girl pupils. Accompanied by one of the girls from the Upper Fifth on the piano, we practised in the Hall during the lunch break.

I am not quite sure whether we were amateur Morris or Country Dancers but our performance entailed a lot of fluttering around the Hall in pairs, in lines or solo.

When we were a little more proficient at it Miss Bean thought it would be a good idea if we performed at the next school concert. She brought yards and yards of butter muslin which she dyed in different pastel shades and made up into diaphanous dresses. We also had wings made of thin wire — these were attached to our backs and also covered with the muslin. Because of the thin nature of the wire, our wings would droop alarmingly after the more energetic parts of the dance. After this lapse of time I cannot recall what we were suppose to represent — angels or fairies perhaps — butterflies maybe? The dyes had not taken very evenly so our dresses were a little blotchy and mottled, but in a dim light this was rather effective. They were however cut rather low in the bodice and showed rather an expanse of underclothes; in the case of Peg and me this meant two or three inches of liberty bodice exposed to the audience! The general effect must have been further marred by our footwear — in every case each pupil was wearing black lace-up plimsolls! Amazing as it may seem, on the night, we received an encore!

At the same concert, Peg and I recited "*The Owl and the Pussycat*". Taking it in turns to recite each verse, we would join together to repeat the last two words of the stanza — this we did with great emphasis.

"*We danced by the light of the Moon*," Peg would say.

"*THE MOON*," we would chorus together.

"*To sell for a shilling your ring*," I would say in a normal voice.

"*YOUR RING*," we would bellow simultaneously.

It must have sounded rather odd to the audience, but I guess that is how we had rehearsed it beforehand. Needless to say, no encore was requested after this.

It was an odd sheltered life in the "Prep" — we were part of the school but a very detached part and had little dealings with the rest of the staff or the elder pupils. Even our morning and afternoon play breaks were at different times, so we had no contact with anyone outside our immediate little circle. We did all meet together for Morning Prayers and when Chasty Apps (the Headmaster) was reading out all the notices, which likewise had very little bearing on small fry like ourselves, we could study the female staff in detail. They sat immediately in front of us, their chairs lined up against the Science room wall. We must have wondered what it would be like when we reached the Second form and they and their subjects would be part of our lives.

Whilst we were being shepherded across the Green by Miss Bean, we would meet these teachers, hurrying to take a lesson in the old school. They would be walking fast — heads thrust forwards and the wide black sleeves of their gowns flapping in the wind. They looked like large, dark birds about to take off in flight and one had the feeling that, if one gave a backward glance, one would see them soaring over the chimney pots out of sight.

CHAPTER
TWO

"On Either Side of the Green"

So we graduated from the cloistered atmosphere of the "Prep" to the Second form. From then on all the rooms in the school would in turn house our particular form.

All the classrooms in the relatively new part of the school were individual, no two precisely alike. Probably the largest and the most interesting was the Science Laboratory. The large wooden table held Bunsen burners and its walls was lined with shelves, crammed with glass containers. Several deep sinks stood under the wide windows. There was always a distinct smell of gas, which combined with that of the chemicals and permeated the atmosphere, seeping out into the Hall when the door was opened.

Opposite was the Lower Fifth room which, because of its position immediately above the boiler room, was the warmest place in the school. Here it was impossible to perch on the radiators during "break", they were always boiling hot in complete contrast with the lukewarm ones elsewhere.

Sandwiched between these two large classrooms were those designated for the Third and Fourth forms, separated from each other with a wooden partition. Maybe because of this it always seemed harder to concentrate in these two rooms. Things happening in the adjoining room could prove a distraction and one could spend a lot of time speculating just what was happening on the other side of the thin boarding. These rooms also bordered Church Street, with large windows looking out onto the street. The noise of the traffic and the chatter from the pavements, filtering up to the open windows in the summer, could also prove distracting.

"If you don't improve in Geometry, my boy," Chasty would say, pointing to a tramp shambling by in front of the fruit shop. "That is how you will end up."

This warning would be repeated whenever he spotted any vagrants in the street beneath. It was not so easy for him to draw comparisons with the girls, although any female gypsy or woman tinker selling clothes pegs or paper flowers called forth the same type of remarks to a lazy girl pupil.

At the other end of the Hall was the Upper Fifth. The pupils here always seemed to be engrossed in work, even when doing "free study" and unattended by a teacher. Maybe this was a front they showed to the rest of the school but, giggling and chattering in the other classrooms, we would wonder if we would reach the exalted heights of the top form.

On wet days the Hall was used for gym — small straw mats were put on the bare boards for floor exercises. Every Tuesday, it was imperative to remember to bring from home one's gym shorts. The penalty for forgetting was to be forced to attend the class in blue knickers and blouses. This omission didn't cause too many problems on a fine day when one could perform in one's underwear in the comparative privacy of the girls' playground. However on a wet day, one could suffer agonies of embarrassment when one's navy bloomers could be seen by any boy pupil passing through the Hall. I can't think why this should have caused us to much agony as, apart from the elastic in the legs, there was not a great deal of difference between these two garments, either in cut or colour!

The girls' cloakrooms always seemed cheerless, with the row of wash hand basins, each with a cold tap, tablet of Windsor soap and roller towel. The row of girls' lavatories commenced with one for the female staff. Strictly out of bounds for the pupils, it was presumably exactly the same as the others, but not one of us would dare to peep inside to find out. I should imagine even in the direst straits one would never dream of entering the "Holy of Holies". The punishment would be far too great!

All the country pupils and those living too far away to go home at midday had sandwiches together in the dinner room, the lofty bleak room in the bottom storey of the old school. Long wooden tables and benches gave it rather a Dickensian appearance.

All the teachers took it in turn to supervise, a task that cannot have been too popular with any of them. After grace, the majority sat reading, immune to the champing of jaws and the chatter around them.

118

We were rather scared of Johnny Haddon, the Chemistry master. He had a thing about the way most of us ate our meal direct from the satchel on our knees.

"Nose bags outside!" he would thunder, his large frame almost filling the doorway. We would all unload our sandwiches hurriedly onto the plates provided. We were to learn later, when he taught us, that Johnny's bark was much worse than his bite and he was in fact quite a "gentle giant".

It was surprising the different types of fillings some of these sandwiches contained — perhaps from choice but more likely from necessity. One girl invariably brought ones made from HP Sauce, which must have got very monotonous after a short while. Perhaps the most uninteresting were the jam sandwiches — especially when the jam was the home-made variety and rather runny. Then it would seep through the butter, staining the bread pink. Combined with crusts that had curled with warmth and age, the resulting sandwich looked revolting. One boy, who probably had a more than usually ingenious mother, would bring beetroot encased in currant bread and butter.

The whole lot would be washed down with cups of cocoa, provided for the sum of one penny a cup. This would be made in large jugs by the prefects. Given exactly the same ingredients, it was surprising how different these brews could be. Sometimes it would be so strong that the powder settled in the bottom of the cup like wet cement. Sometimes it was predominately milk, quite often too sweet, although on occasions the sugar had been entirely forgotten. However it was

119

normally warm and therefore quite welcome on a cold winter's day. In the summer, the more affluent of the "Dinner Children" brought cubes of solidified fizzy lemonade which when dissolved in cold water produced a drink rather like fruit flavoured liver salts.

Domestic Science and Wood Work were taught in the old part of the school. The boys hammered and banged away in the large wood strewn classroom beyond the dinner room, whilst the girls cooked and sewed at the other end of the building. A row of gas ovens lined one wall of the Domestic Science room, whilst long scrubbed work tables and forms were on the other side. Here we cooked sausage rolls, cheese straws, fairy cakes and jam tarts, with varying degrees of success.

There were always enthusiastic customers for our cooking, no matter how badly it turned out. The boys returning from the Woodwork lesson would plead, cajole, and finally intimidate us into parting with it. They even gobbled up with relish some doughnuts that had turned out like lumps of greasy dough. Our respective mothers must have wondered why, although we left on Friday mornings with all the necessary raw ingredients, we rarely returned with the finished products.

CHAPTER
THREE

Prizes & Parties

The Town Hall was hired for the Annual Prize Giving or Speech Day, the School Hall did not possess a stage nor was it large enough to accommodate all the visitors.

These events all followed the same pattern — only the Guest Speaker varied as did the length of speech he made before the presentation and his remarks to the prizewinners. As far as I remember, it was always a male who officiated, quite often an old boy of the school who had made a distinguished career for himself after leaving school.

Seated at the back of the stage, all the teaching staff looked a trifle strange and unreal. We put it down to the fact that were all wearing their best gowns, gone were the rusty black ones we were so familiar with in the classrooms, the ones that were normally covered with chalk marks and, in the case of Johnny Haddon, the chemistry master, also riddled with holes due to too close contact with acid and the Bunsen burners! In their place were elegant gowns with fur trimming and, in some cases, sporting gaily coloured lining to the sleeves. If the teachers looked different, not so the School Governors, who never seemed to vary from one

121

year to the next. They must have differed over the years but, from the floor of the Hall, they looked exactly the same. Amongst their numbers there would be at least one elderly woman with a flowery hat, who would sit gazing into the distance over our heads, a fixed smile on her face. The Mayor was normally there, he and the Mayoress wearing their chains of office. Some of the Governors would be motionless throughout the proceedings, looking as if they might drop off to sleep at any second; others would fidget and stir uneasily on their hard chairs throughout Chasty's speech of welcome.

With clarity I can remember one of our first Speech Days. Dick, who had left school, was coming back to claim his prize for passing School Certificate. Barbara had won her form prize, whilst Peg and I had the doubtful glory of jointly winning the Nature Study Prize for the Preparatory form. In deference to this, never to be repeated, event Mother had hired a car to take us all into Calne. We were ready and waiting in good time for Mr A. I. Hillier to come to collect us. Time was getting short, however, when Mr Hillier drove quickly up, reversed sharply into the yard, and jumped from the driving seat of his thirty-seater bus. As he held the door for us to scramble aboard, he explained that his car had a puncture, so he had no choice but to use his bus.

The five of us sat in different parts of the large vehicle and tried to look as if we were fee-paying passengers on a service bus. However nonchalant we might have appeared, we felt decidedly odd and hoped that none of our friends would witness our arrival on the Strand.

Because we were to share the Nature Study prize, Miss Bean, in one of the sentimental moods, thought it would be suitable if Peg and I walked hand in hand onto the stage to receive it. She had reckoned without the rickety steps that led from the floor to the platform and which would only accommodate single file traffic. Peg and I started off all right but got separated at the steps and never really got together again. I think the poor prize giver got hopelessly muddled at being confronted with two recipients for "The Illustrated Book of British Birds"! In the end, Peg was handed the prize and he shook me limply by the hand in rather an abstracted sort of way.

We heaved a sigh of relief on leaving the Town Hall to see that Mr Hillier was waiting for us at the wheel of his "Austin", the puncture mended!

The school parties were held on two consecutive nights in early December, the first one for the Preparatory and the first two forms in the upper school, the second one for the rest of the school. The Junior party was from 7.00 till 9.00p.m. and the Seniors continuing until the giddy hour of 10.00p.m.

To save the bike journey to and from Stockley after school, Peg and I would go to tea with our best friend, Dorothy Leavesley, whose home was in London Road. We would leave our party dresses at Dorothy's house in the morning *en route* for school and change into them from our gymslips in the evening.

123

The School parties all followed the same pattern, the same games, even the same eats, and I can't think why we enjoyed them so much as we did. Maybe it was because the teachers lost all their stiffness and really put their hearts and souls into entertaining themselves and us. We played rhyming games, games with balloons and those that entailed "dressing up". We rehearsed in secret, behind the bike sheds, the words we would use in charades, fiercely driving away would-be onlookers who might spy out the words we were going to use. The eats were as predictable as the entertainment. Sandwiches cut and filled in the domestic Science room by Miss Stephens and the girls from the Upper Fifth, plus fancy cakes from Maslen's Café, all washed down by gallons of orangeade. All that remained after the parties was taken by the prefects to the old people in the Almshouses. The last winter at school Peg and I helped to distribute the food.

We walked along the pavement, past the Green Dragon Public House to the Almshouses and tapped on all the thick black doors, which opened directly onto the narrow pavement. The tiny windows had latticed panes which let in a modicum of light, so that their little living rooms seemed to be in perpetual twilight. I found this strangely depressing, perhaps it was seeing so many aged folk at one time. They seemed very cheerful however and were delighted with the iced cakes.

CHAPTER
FOUR

Playtime & Sports

The girls' playground was "L shaped" and followed the contours of the school buildings. The perimeter of the expanse of asphalt had as its boundary a high wire fence. In the high wooden fence that separated the playground from Church Street was a large horse chestnut tree, its spreading branches stretching out over the street as well as shading part of the school buildings.

This tree always seemed to be shedding something — its creamy white blossoms in early summer, followed by a shower of conkers in the autumn. Finally the early winter gales would bring the golden leaves swirling down to drift into dirty heaps until they were swept away by the caretaker. We would use the trunk as a wicket during lunchtime games of cricket. In a heatwave, it would be pleasant under its dappled shade.

Not far from the tree there were steps leading down to an iron gate which opened directly into Church Street. This gate was always kept locked and used, as far as I knew, by Chasty Apps when he made his daily journey across the road to Maslen's Café for his lunch. Everyone else used the entrance from the Green.

Stray balls would have a habit of bouncing down these steps and under the gate into the road — it was one of the deadlier sins to enlist the help of "passers by" in returning the errant balls. Errand boys whistling by on their bikes, their large wicker basket full of groceries or meat, were always willing to assist. Leaving their bikes leaning against the cycle shop window, they would hurl the balls back with excellent aim. Unfortunately this was generally the time when Chasty was either *en route* or returning from Maslen's. Even when we had worked out that he was probably only half way through the first course, one was never quite sure if he wasn't peering through a window, over the rows of lardies and cream cakes.

On the whole it was easier to play ball games in the part of the playground near the Green. Here one could get interrupted by girls pushing their bikes through to the bicycle sheds, but at least one didn't have all the trouble of lost balls.

Quite often the "Stop me and buy one" Ice Cream salesman would ride his cycle slowly over the Green and stop by the school railings. For one penny we bought large three sided fruit ices and, if one was really wealthy, a cream ice for two pence.

The games field was some distance from the school. We would set off in an untidy crocodile across the Green and turn down into the gloom of Horsebrook. Here the smell of wild garlic would filter over the high stone wall which flanked the right hand pavement and mingle with the smell which emitted from the Gas Works, making this part of Calne particularly odorous.

Opposite the massive Iron Foundry Works were several small grimy cottages, their doors, like those of a stable, opening in two parts. Whenever we clattered by, at one of those doors would frequently be standing a woman. She wore a hessian sack tied around her black skirt and she looked poor, dirty and sad. Framed in the dark doorway, with the cobbled pavement in front, she could have stepped straight from the nineteenth century.

These tiny cottages with their broken windows were such a contrast to the elegant three storey houses on the Green. Here the large Georgian windows would be half shuttered against the afternoon sun, but in Horsebrook the tiny broken casement windows seemed to be in perpetual twilight.

I was always pleased to climb the bank into Anchor Road where we turned off into a cinder track, which led to the playing field. The field held two tennis courts fenced in with netting, a pavilion and ample room for hockey, cricket and football pitches. Most of the time six or seven sheep grazed around the hedges and fences.

Because of the distance between the field and the school, it was quite possible to start off in brilliant sunshine but before one had got started with games, rain would be falling steadily. In this case we sheltered in or under the pavilion, undecided if it was "in for the day" or just a passing shower. On sports days the field would look much smaller with the influx of proud parents and friends. The visitors sat on long forms and watched the races which started with the young pupils

127

and gradually, as the afternoon wore on, graduated to the Upper Fifth and Sixth. One thing for sure, Fitzmaurice House, the House to which Peg and I belonged, would be sure to finish last. Throughout our schooling it never excelled either academically or in the sport fields. Lansdowne and Priestly always seemed to be in front. Perhaps it improved after we left!

Several long back gardens belonging to a row of cottages in Anchor Road bordered one of the fences of the field. A wild cricket ball would sometimes land in one of these back gardens. Normally it was no trouble to get it back, there was always some willing person to throw it over the hedge. Not so if it pitched in the garden belonging to one old couple.

Their back garden held geese, who rushed at intruders, hissing loudly and with outspread wings. On realising that one of the school's balls was nestling among her cabbages, the old lady, rather like one of her geese, would dash down the garden path, her old fashioned sunbonnet on the back of her head and her print frock flapping round her legs. It took a brave player to face her wrath.

Apparently Chasty Apps had once hit a ball into this forbidden territory. The rest of the team watched with interest as, with dignified tread, he went to retrieve his ball. Ignoring the fact that he was the Headmaster, she let forth the same stream of abuse that she normally showered on the lesser fry.

The games field was also the venue for the eliminating heats for the Area School Sports, when the competitors from all the Calne County Schools met to decide who would represent the town at the County Sports at Trowbridge.

Peg normally gained a place in most events for her age group — I did not excel at field sports, but one year I unexpectedly scraped through to a place in the 220 yards, reaching the finishing line with bursting lungs and on the point of collapse. It didn't do me a great deal of good. Unfortunately on the day, one of my fellow runners fell in front of me and I finished last.

Each Wiltshire town had its own distinctive colours — our black shorts and yellow striped vests gave us the nickname of "The Calne Bumble Bees". This sport gear was distributed amongst the chosen competitors about a week before the event. A rough survey was made of your measurements and you were allotted a set approximately suited to one's height and girth. It was all right if one was more or less stock size but any child with unusual statistics could look most odd. It was generally felt that the shorts were far too long in the leg, in most cases they came just below the knee. The hurdlers and high jumpers found them most restricting. One year some the girls daringly altered them the night before so that as well as looking more modern, they allowed for more freedom of movement. The alterations were not noticed until they were ready to perform by which time it was too late for the hems to be let down again.

Before the first event, all the competitors marched around the large oval sports arena. As the representatives from each town drew level with the grandstand, with heads turned sideways they gave the Olympic

Salute to Lord Burghley, who always officiated from the spectators' seats. This could look quite impressive, especially from the spectators' seats. One could sit there, sucking an ice cream and eagerly anticipate the events of the afternoon. On the other hand, those taking part were full of apprehension as they faced the ordeals of the track. Apart from anything else, they had only been allowed a frugal lunch as Miss Salter, who was in charge of the girl competitors, was convinced that one ran at one's fastest on a really empty stomach!

Records were made and broken and it all seemed terribly important at the time. Coming home in the bus, the whole afternoon would be relived — heated arguments breaking out now and again as to the results of such and such a race. If by some chance athletes from the school had been chosen to represent Wiltshire at Stamford Bridge, it was a time for rejoicing and a mention from Chasty the next morning at prayers.

CHAPTER
FIVE

"Music Hath Charms . . ."

Just about the time we started in the Second form, Peg and I began piano lessons. Every Thursday afternoon, during the dinner hour, between 1p.m. and 2p.m., we went to Miss Ada Blackford's home in Shelburne Road. Ada had quite a few pupils from the school. Barbara had also been a pupil of hers for several years, her musical abilities about matching mine — being practically non-existent.

When it became apparent the Peg had all the ability, Ada made her own arrangements as to how the hour should be divided up. In the end, Peg would have forty minutes, while I wrestled with Ezra Read's Pianoforte Tutor for a mere twenty minutes. This suited me admirably. I would much prefer to sit in the comfort of Ada's chintzy armchair and listen to Peg performing than practise scales myself. To give Ada her due, she did once try to teach us *The Marche Militaire* as a duet. I would thump away on the same two easy chords in the left hand, while Peg played all the intricate treble parts. In spite of the simplicity of my part, I could never quite catch up and was always a bar or so behind.

131

Miss Blackford's sitting room walls was a taxidermist's delight. In glass cases there were all sorts of stuffed birds, perched realistically on the gnarled boughs of trees. Pride of place went to a fox, who held in its mouth a stoat. The stoat's look of frozen terror and the sly cunning in the eyes of its captor seemed to portray the brutality of Nature.

On a hot summer afternoon, the cream blinds with their green silk lining would be half drawn against the sun's rays. Then, in the resulting half-green light, the room took on a different, rather eerie, aspect altogether. Sunk deep in the armchair, with eyes half closed, it was almost as if I was transported to some tropical rain forest. The humble stuffed thrushes and wood pigeons became exotic birds of paradise and the fox some wild beast carrying its prey through the undergrowth. Then the strains of Peg playing and the sound of Ada gently beating time to the music would bring me back to reality.

Hung in a prominent position on the walls between the glass cases was a large double bass. Both Peg and I wondered if diminutive little Ada could ever have played this enormous intrument. We tried in vain to visualise her tiny legs straddling the base of the instrument while her short arms held the long bow. Perhaps it belonged to another member of the family — we didn't think to ask.

Just how long it took Mother to realise that I should never make a pianist, I'm not sure. Peg, by this time, was making enormous progress and could even master the organ. In fact Mother bought a second-hand

American organ for ten pounds from the second-hand shop in Church Street so that she could practise at home.

Whether Mother felt that we should both be treated alike, or whether she thought that given the right instrument I would be just as musical, I don't know. However from a Chippenham shop she bought me a banjo. I am also not sure if Ada was approached about teaching me to play the thing. If she was, I guess she declined, for Mother elicited the help of the school's part-time violin teacher.

I cannot now remember her name, but she was an elderly lady with greying hair, which was parted in the middle and plaited in coils around each ear, rather like headphones. Each coil was kept in place with large black jet hatpins, which looked very much like the currants in two large Chelsea buns.

During two dinner hours a week, she taught the violin to aspiring musicians. Judging from the wails which wafted over the girls' playground from the open windows of the Fifth form, some of her pupils' prowess at the violin equalled mine at the piano. She was, however, quite a good teacher, but faced with the banjo and me as a pupil must have been quite a challenge.

I don't think it was an instrument she had had any dealings with before, and I rather suspect that she thumbed through the tutor two pages in front of me before each lesson. Every Tuesday dinnertime, we stumbled through "*Oh Susannah*" and "*The Camptown Races*" with little success.

Eventually, much to the elderly lady's relief, the whole venture was abandoned. The banjo was relegated to a shelf in the box room where it may still be for all I know.

Peg started playing the organ at church. This caused me quite a lot of unnecessary worry at the beginning. I don't know why as she proved very competent from the start. For the first few services, I suffered agonies, scared that she would go wrong in the psalms, terrified that she would miscalculate the number of verses in the hymns, and either stop short whilst everyone was singing or, worse, carry on solo in a silent church. I can't remember any major mistakes — I should of course have been blissfully ignorant of a few wrong notes.

Singing lessons at school was taken by Mr Pullein, a church organist. He was very musical and must have suffered agonies trying to coach some sort of harmony from eighty per cent of his pupils. He had a small goatee beard which resulted in his nickname "Nanny".

For an elderly man he was very agile. He would leap from the music stool and stride around the Hall conducting *"Oh Danube Blue"* with one hand, his head a little to one side, trying to catch anyone singing "off key". Invariably I was one of the culprits and I soon found out that I was more of an hindrance than a help to the class. I went through a phase when I silently mouthed the words, no discordant notes issuing from my mouth. In the end I gave up the unequal struggle, expelled myself from the class and every Friday afternoon went to help mark out the hockey pitch. According to the rest of the class, "Nanny" never enquired as to my whereabouts!

CHAPTER
SIX

School Friends

We found many mutual friends at school. They had to be friends with both of us. We didn't split up and have our own individual chums. Consequently, as time went by, we shared with Dorothy, Eileen, Audrey, Joan, Freda and several others the beauty of Stockley Woods in bluebell time and Kings Play on a hot summer evening. We both had this undiminishing love of the downs.

One summer holiday, Peg and I together with two of these friends from school planned a long hike from Kings Play to the Cherhill Monument and back. For days we discussed just which day we would undertake this mammoth walk, just what we should need in the way of food and drink etc.

The chosen day, at the beginning of August, turned out to be one of glorious weather. There was a slight haze over the downs and the poppies were blazing at the side of Heddington Hollow as, quite early in the morning, we walked up the narrow chalk lane. Before we reached the top, we cut across the fields towards Kings Play. The turf, cropped close by the sheep, was dotted with the bright blue of harebells and the peewits

135

soared across the clear sky, calling with sad haunting cries.

We made the mistake of including several large bottles of lemonade with our food. These we found far too weighty to carry around for long, so we sat at the very top of Kings Play and drank the contents of a couple of bottles to lessen the load.

We attempted to take the shortest possible route to the Monument. It didn't look too far away as we viewed it from the side of Fox Covers, but we had reckoned without the rolling downlands. Struggling up to the summit and then running down the other side of each incline seemed to double the distance. By the time we had reached Blackland Hollow, our legs were getting tired and, in the full blast of the midday sun, we could have done with the lemonade that we had drunk so recklessly at the start of our journey.

The tall Monument gradually loomed nearer and nearer until, at along last, we were stood practically underneath the lofty column. Nearby was the giant White Horse. The four of us ate the remainder of our sandwiches sitting on its enormous sloping eye. We could see the traffic moving slowly and sedately along the Cherhill Road like children's toys on the grey ribbon of the road. The White Horse Garage (demolished in 1999) looking as if it was also a child's plaything, with toy petrol pumps and miniature fir trees lining the road side.

The hot afternoon slipped by so quickly and the sun was already low in the sky when we left. We cheated somewhat on the way home and missed going home via

Kings Play. We crossed the road by the Golf Course, where one solitary golfer was wearily climbing out of a bunker in the fading light, and took the short cut to Stockley down Violet Lane. Here the branches of the trees met and intertwined into a leafy ceiling, shutting out the last of the daylight. It was chilly when the sun had disappeared in a blaze of orange sky.

When we reached the farm, footsore and tired, our two stoical friends still had the cycle ride to Calne to face. We waved them off as they pedalled wearily up the road towards the Knapp.

Peg and I rarely had a Birthday party. Rightly or wrongly, Mother thought that it would appear that we were asking for presents. However, we did once hold a Birthday party for Samuel Sebastian, my old black tom cat, to which we invited some of our school friends. We felt fairly sure of his age — fourteen, but not quite certain of the actual date. Mother thought that May was the month. This was probably correct as it was well known that "May kittens were no good" and Sam had never proved to be one of life's workers!

At the party, Freda Taylor, whose parents had a wet fish shop in Calne, arrived with half a pound of best cod for the birthday cat. Mother cooked it during the afternoon and, while we were having our own tea, Sam wolfed the lot. It must have seemed sheer luxury after a lifetime of sharing heads and bones from the family's kippers.

After his large meal, Sam went to sleep under the white lilac trees by the road, his tummy extended by his enormous repast, his battle-scarred face resting on his thin paws.

We never risked a birthday party for Chum, the family dog. He was far too anti-social and had changed rapidly from a small fluffy bundle of mischief to a lean rather irritable cattle dog. Devoted to the family, he however soon established a reputation for not being particularly friendly towards anyone else, especially pedestrians and cyclists passing the farm. Unlike Jock, our previous dog, he was not very fond of children and we would have to forestall any that rushed to "pat the nice doggie". To stumble over him when he was asleep was to court disaster as he wasn't above giving his nearest and dearest a nip should this happen. We were forever making excuses for him.

"Chum is so highly strung," Mother would sigh.

We blamed his indiscretions on "his nerves", "the heat of July" or the fact that something had upset him. He was easily upset — the distant sound of the Hunt, even when they were fields away, would guarantee several hours of continuous barking from Chum. Seated in the yard, he would keep it up for ages, only stopping when his throat became too sore to continue.

He was also a persistent roamer, one lady friend at Tossels Farm and another at Rookery Farm meant that quite a lot of his time was divided between the two of them. As we were not on the telephone, news would circulate via Pet Smith that Chum was at one or the other and someone would set off across the fields to collect him. Unrepentant, he would stay at home for a short while until the opportunity arose when he could slope off across the fields unobserved. However, all this had absolutely nothing to do with school friends, I seem to have wandered away from the Chapter heading!

During our last few years at school, there were twenty four children in the form — nineteen boys and five girls. Presum, because of our proportionally smaller numbers, there was generally quite a feud between the two sexes. I suppose we had to assert ourselves at times or we would have had no voice whatsoever in the running of the form.

On rare occasions a note would be passed from some amorous boy to one of "the five". This would be handed around between the girls and the resulting answer a joint effort composed by all of us during the break. Generally this took place behind the cycle shed. I don't think it was at all as the sender intended.

The boys were given to strange fads, which lasted for a few weeks and could prove quite amusing. Any variation in dress was frowned upon by the Hierarchy and school uniform had to be strictly adhered to. Consequently they had to find other ways to express their individuality.

For some weeks it was "the thing" for them to appear in class with the front lock of their hair sporting one enormous wave. This the local barber achieved for them. It cost an additional penny when they had a trim. The deep corrugations gradually became shallower and shallower until, through length of time and the application of Brylcream, they gradually faded

139

altogether leaving the owner's hair uniformly straight all over.

Another time "snuff taking" became quite popular. Each boy haunted the local junk shop and bought themselves snuffboxes — some of them old and interesting antiques. The boys had all the correct mannerisms, tapping the lid delicately with two fingers before opening up and indulging. This habit went on for several months but came to an abrupt end during a Physics lesson. One addict foolishly took an extra large sniff during the lesson which resulted in streaming eyes and prolonged sneezing, which drew Johnny Haddon's attention to the miscreant. All the snuffboxes were then confiscated — I wonder if they were returned to the owners. Collectively they would be worth a fortune at today's prices.

I know little of what happened to the boys of our form. One, who was frequently threatened by Chasty with the prospects of becoming a vagrant, became I believe, a Barrister of note.

"You will be completely dependhent of the generwosity of others," Chasty would lisp. How wrong he was!

Others probably did just as well. I imagined most of them would have served in the forces during the Second World War. The girls we saw more frequently, although it would be years between each meeting. Then we would remark on "How the children had grown", and "How time flies", yet it would seem an eternity since we shared our lessons and indeed our lives in the old school buildings on The Green.

CHAPTER SEVEN

Bikes

People cycled miles in those pre-war years and bicycles seemed to be the most important possessions to the majority of folk, irrespective of their age or occupation.

School transport started while we were attending school, but it only applied to the Secondary Modern pupils. They had no luxury bus however — theirs was a windowless van with an open back and a tailboard. The tailboard let down revealing a set of steps which the passengers used to get in and out of the conveyance. Apart from the open back, it resembled a "Black Maria". As we pedalled along, it would pass us, the two rows of children facing each other in the dim interior. If there was a force eight gale blowing and the driving rain was making our faces raw, it seemed a most enviable way of travelling.

The worst rains always seemed to occur when we were wearing our Panama hats. The upturned brims would hold a certain amount and then a gutter would form, throwing a cascade of icy water down the necks of our blouses. We tried all ways to rejuvenate these Panama hats — starching them; cleaning them by means of spirit and an old tooth brush, pressing the brims with a warm iron, but they always looked limp and discoloured after they got really wet. One enterprising girl "*blancoed*" hers, but with the first shower of rain her navy blazer looked as if it has been whitewashed.

Saturday nights would see the road to Calne quite busy with two-wheel traffic. Young folk off to the flicks (this was the cinema which stood where Somerfields now stands in Calne) or a Town Hall Dance. Lone men, dressed in their best were and sporting a seasonable buttonhole, were allowed out for a pint and a natter among their own sex. Independent of public transport, they cycled on their stout framed Raleigh and Hercules machines, free-wheeling down hills and puffing up all the inclines. Sometimes a whole family set off for a ride, Mother, with the youngest strapped firmly onto a cushion on the carrier. Dad would have the next eldest either on the handlebars or the cross bar and the rest of the children following on small bikes of their own.

I have seen workman carrying scythes, axes and billhooks strapped along the crossbar on the way to their work. One could envisage the most gory results if there had been an accident. Our chimney sweep carried the tools of his trade in this way, the thick bundle of rods extending from handlebars to saddle, with the sooty brush sticking out even further beyond the back wheel, like a propeller.

The chimney sweep with the name of Mr A. Little, lived in Calne. His name was rather a misnomer as he was quite a plump man with a round smiling face. As we had no telephone, we had to visit his home in

Anchor Road to make an appointment. His talkative wife would get out her soot stained notebook to "Book us in". She would sit on the doorstep and make pencil entries on the grey pages — we often wondered how she deciphered the bookings afterwards. She would talk all the time and her black hair would escape from the hatpins and fall about her face.

Mrs Little would often confuse Mother with Auntie Win from Beversbrook. I suppose this was understandable, as there was a decided family likeness. On two separate times, we had been waiting at home, dust sheets over the furniture and the house in a state of disarray. In the meantime, Mr Little had pedalled, on his brush laden bike, from Calne to Beversbrook and surprised Auntie Win with his unexpected visit. On another occasion the situation had been reversed. It was during the height of an "Indian Summer", when the September sun seemed as hot or hotter than that of midsummer. We were just starting off to pick blackberries as Mr Little cycled into the yard at the precise time that he should have been arriving at Beversbrook. Mother, feeling sorry that he had wasted the journey, hurriedly swept the vases and ornaments from the dining room mantelpiece, rolled back the carpets and let him sweep that chimney, on the assumption that it would need doing before the winter in any case!

So bikes were everywhere. Propped against the lych-gate and beneath the churchyard hedges for Sunday services, leant one against the other in untidy rows in fields adjoining local flower shows and fêtes and propped precariously by the pedals against pavements in towns. Front lamps, pump and tool kits vanished frequently from unattended machines and one could be unfortunate enough to lose the entire bike if one didn't take the precaution of chaining the spokes to the mud guard!

CHAPTER EIGHT

Senior Citizens

"The Elderly Inhabitants of Stockley" — thus read one of the headings in the local weekly paper. Then followed a description of some of the senior citizens and a surmise that the village must be an extremely healthy place in which to spend one's retirement. Apparently in the mid 1930s the over-sixties far outnumbered the children and the middle-aged. We had not fully realised this interesting fact; it took a zealous reporter and half a page coverage in the *Wiltshire Gazette* to bring it home to us.

In the row of cottages near the farm, there were a number of elderly people. Tom Paget and his wife I have described in detail in a previous chapter. Next door to them in a minute two up and two down cottage lived Mrs Surmon, a widow. Mrs Surmon and the Pagets were never the best of friends — I do not rightly know just how the quarrel started, I believe it was something to do with their jointly owned wall. It was probably such a long time ago that the participants had forgotten how hostilities started! We visited Mrs Surmon with the Parish Magazine. She kept herself very much to herself and her main interest seemed to be her only daughter. Once a barmaid in the White Hart, Calne, she had married a man with money and position and quite understandably was of chief importance in her Mother's life and her main topic of conversation.

Next door to her lived old Mrs Marvin and elderly Annie Summers rented a cottage a couple of doors from that. So within a quarter of a mile there were several octogenarians or ones heading that way!

Quite a long way from attaining that age but nevertheless retired and living at Elm Hurst, Stockley, were the Eatwells. Everything was so neat in their home, furniture was polished until it gleamed and nothing seemed out of place or untidy. The garden was weed free, the front lawn clipped and edged with meticulous care. There were circular flowerbeds of begonias; when it was hot and dry, the brightly coloured blooms would drop. Mrs Eatwell would put them in shallow bowls on the dining room table, where they looked like exotic water lilies. The Eatwells had no children of their own but, each summer, a lively young niece, Margaret Cornell, would come to stay with them for the summer holidays. She was about the age of Peg and me and the three of us became firm friends.

Although living in Manchester, she took to the country life as if she was born and bred to it. The beginning of August would see her haring down to the farm on her skinny legs like a tornado and we would start where we had left off the previous summer — exploring the downs, riding round the village on our bikes or roaming the fields. After a few weeks she was gone — back to the city. With a country dweller's dislike of town life, we wondered how she could bear it.

Uncle Harry and Auntie Edie Pocock both came under the title of "elderly", although Auntie Edie was rather annoyed at being described in the paper as "a few years younger than her husband". This for her rather soured the thrill of making the headlines! Next door to them lived Mr and Mrs Tom Chivers. Tom had worked at Church Farm and had many tales to tell of his life there as a boy. Plump Mrs Little at the shop, old Mrs Strange and Mr and Mrs Harry Huband from West View Cottages were others. Mrs Huband's fine unlined skin and her serene blue eyes would have done justice to a woman half her age.

Jacob Summers lived nearby. At one time he had worked at Whetham Farm. We were rather scared of him but I don't quite know why. It probably all stemmed from the fact that he had once caught Dick at the top of one of his damson trees. Barbara, who I suspect had suggested the raid on the damson tree in the first place, showing rather a cowardly streak, ran away and hid behind the tool shed. Under cover of the twilight, Dick shinned down the tree and escaped but for months after the event, neither of them could be sure if they had been recognised and if so, whether or not Jacob would tell the family. This should not have worried Peg and me as we were not involved in any way, but the sight of Jacob's stocky figure and bearded face would strike terror into our hearts!

Mr and Mrs Bullock lived in part of Mrs and Mrs Arthur Hunt's house at Stockley. They had come from

147

London and must have found the depth of the country such a contrast to city life. Peg and I would spend part of Saturday afternoon sitting with them in their little front room. They were a tiny childless little couple with a great love and understanding for children. I wish I had written down of their remembrances of Edwardian London. Eventually Mr Bullock died and his widow lived on alone — we still went to see her. As we got larger, she seemed to shrink until she appeared like a miniature period doll with her black alpaca dress with its rows of tiny seed pearls around the neckline.

Mrs Hatter lived in the "Pillar Box" cottages — an ugly name for a row of pretty thatched houses whose long gardens stretched away into the distance from a paved path. The neat rows of vegetables bordered by narrow grass paths seemed to go on forever. On a Sunday afternoon, Mrs Hatter would always have one or more of her daughters visiting her. "The Hatter Girls," Mother still called them although they were all grown up and married.

Heddington, although not given the same publicity, also had some interesting old people. In the early 1920s when the threshing machine would travel from farm to farm at Harvest time, Mrs Grubb would travel with it and work with the farm hands as a casual labourer. Although not a young woman, she would stand on the corn stack and throw the heavy sheaves onto the top of the threshing machine. When she came down from the stack, she would shake her long black skirt and the mice that had bolted there for safety would scurry away! Peg and I who had inherited Mother's aversion to both rats and mice were appalled at this story.

Whatever she did, Mrs Grubb seemed to do at great speed. With long strides, she could cover the road between Heddington and Stockley, pushing her granddaughter, Joyce, in her pram. We would see her in the distance, just passing Willowbrook and, within seconds, she was level with our garden gate. The old pram would rock backwards and forwards and Joyce's small head would bob up and down so that it would seem likely that she might swallow the soother that dangled from her mouth. Always in a hurry, Mrs Grubb once explained to us that she couldn't stop as "she had put some fat in the oven to 'verify it'." She quite often got her vocabulary a bit mixed.

Mrs Holmes, the mother of Alfie, the village carrier, ran the Little Heddington shop on the Turnpike Road. Apparently one summer afternoon, one of the Rector's young daughters had, suddenly and unexpectedly, been sick all over Mrs Holme's clean flagstone floor. From that day forward, all children had been prohibited from crossing her threshold. This seemed a little harsh, as the chances of another such unfortunate accident seemed most remote. Grown-ups, presumably because they could be relied upon to behave with more self-control, could shop from the inside, but all transactions with the children took place on the path outside.

Kids with pennies and half pennies clutched in their hands viewed the rows of sweet bottles through the window and made their selection from the pear drops, gob stoppers, bull's eyes and liquorice boot laces displayed there. Sales were transacted by shouting to Mrs Holmes through the open doorway and goods and money passed hands outside in the sunshine. This practice seemed to have been carried on for years.

The Miss Knowlers were two elderly spinsters living at Heddington. They were always together and looked rather like miniature copies of Queen Mary, with their little toques (a close-fitting cap, bonnet or head-dress worn by men and women at various periods), their long black coats with fur collars and their tall umbrellas. They kept house for their brother, Woodland Knowler. Peg and I found this Christian name peculiar — we rather expected him to resemble Robin Hood but he didn't!

There was also a niece, Susie, who they all looked after with a fierce possessiveness. Although she looked almost as elderly as her aunts, they would vet the library books collected from the school each week, just in case there might be an objectionable word not fit for Susie's eyes.

"I do not allow Susie to go to the WC in the winter," Minnie the elder sister told the Rector as she poured him a second cup of tea one November afternoon. The poor man was quite mystified and not a little alarmed until he realised that she was referring to the WI and had got her abbreviations somewhat mixed!

CHAPTER
NINE

The Younger Fry

There was a youth in the Village, however, although the enthusiastic reporter from the Wiltshire Gazette made it seem as if Stockley was peopled entirely by ancients.

The first grandchild of the Ruddle family arrived at the little bungalow at the foot of Stockley Hollow. Peg and I were allowed to push brown-eyed Barbara Ann out for walks in her low, small-wheeled pram. Apprehensively at first and scared that the baby might cry and that we should be unable to cope, we kept to the roads of the Hollow. Both pushing hard on the handles, we would struggle up the steep incline, past Freddie Summer's garden to the Chalk Pits. Then we turned and walked as far as the Knapp in the other direction, always keeping in sight the spiralling smoke from the Bungalow chimney. She rarely cried however, so we ventured further afield, picking flowers from the hedgerows while the small occupant in the pram watched us with eyes solemn and unblinking beneath her white pixie hood. Later on, we pushed out her cousin Harvey. By this time older and more responsible, we took him down to the Farm and became quite adept at undoing the safety straps and carrying him to play on the lawn.

Harvey's parents had a new Ford car. Black and shiny with gleaming wheels and, if I recollect correctly, the first model they marketed at the amazingly low price of one hundred pounds. We felt it was the last word in elegance. Quite a lot of people we knew had older cars, but none of them had anything quite as modern a this square bodied sparkling four seater. We went for drives with them on Sunday evenings and hoped fervently that we should meet lots of people we knew as we bowled along the country roads!

Heddington too had its fair share of youth, especially when the Arrowsmith family came to live there. Mr Arrowsmith ran the racing stables and his large family filled to overflowing the bungalow at The Beeches. There were nine or ten children, ranging in age from late twenties down to twins of four years old. They were a happy extrovert family, predominately girls with just two boys. They adored their Mother, who must have spent the best part of her life feeding and clothing such a horde of children. They were somewhat in awe of their father who was very strict.

Whatever age one had attained there always seemed to be an Arrowsmith of similar years with whom to be friends. Peg and I became friends with Jean and Iris, while Barbara soon struck a friendship with Evie.

By this time Barbara had grown up and started to teach. She became quite clothes conscious and with the aid of Mother's old sewing machine made herself summer dresses of sparva and tobralco (cotton materials of that time), totally different from gymslips and school uniform. All this combined with make-up and a seven and sixpenny perm made her seem quite grown-up and enviable in our eyes. With her self-made wardrobe she became independent of Auntie Kate's clothes parcels which now became the prerogative of Peg and me entirely!

With rather dazzling flowery material, Barbara made herself beach pyjamas — they were in vogue at the time. However Dad decreed that they were not to be worn in public. Peg and I thought this a great shame as they looked so modern and attractive. However I suppose the wearing of them would be the equivalent of going "topless" in this day and age!

Peg and I was probably quite a nuisance when it came to Barbara's boy friends. We didn't exactly do any stalking but we always seemed to be in the wrong place at the wrong moment. We would happen to be strolling up Violet Lane *en route* for the Golf Course, or else climbing the slippery slopes of Kings Play, at the very moment they happened along. With scant tact, we hung around, obviously not wanted but impervious to loaded hints and even threats.

We were most intrigued by one of these fleeting boyfriends — he was Canadian, I believe. Peg and I christened him "Hank" although that was obviously not his name. He made the great mistake of calling us "Those terrible twins" in our hearing and, far from being subdued by this, we were delighted and rather flattered. It made us feel rather on a par with the fictional characters in "*The Terrors of the Lower Fifth*" and we became even more of a nuisance.

One warm midsummer Barbara and Evie Arrowsmith camped out for two nights in a tent at the top of Stockley Hollow. This seemed to us the height of sophistication. The tent was pitched near the hunting gate, which led over the fields to Kings Play. We walked up there to visit them on the first night they pitched their tent. They made us two cups of rather smoky tea but I can't recall that we were offered anything to eat. I suppose one could not blame them as all their gear and food had been lugged with a great deal of effort up the steep slopes of the Hollow on their bikes. We noticed with interest that Barbara was wearing the controversial beach pyjamas.

Not far from the Arrowsmiths', lived the Drews. Albie Drew was a roadman or lengthman who, together with Tommy Gartside, swept the roads and trimmed the verges of the village. He lived in a little thatched cottage in Hamsley Hollow. He was short and plump and had a slight impediment in his speech, which made it difficult for him to pronounce certain letters.

When the roads needed resurfacing, Tommy and Albie were joined by a gang of council workmen with their steamroller. This giant machine, its brass glittering in the sunshine, would make sudden little spurts of speed up and down the freshly laid tar and chippings, thick smoke belching from its chimney. At these times, Albie and Tommy acted as lookouts to warn the gang of approaching traffic.

"Tupple of Tar Tumming," Albie shouted one summer afternoon as two cars rounded the corner by the Post Office.

Albie's wife rather resembled him in build and stature but between them they had produced a beautiful daughter — Gwennie. Their only child, she must indeed have been the apple of their eyes. Her golden hair, blue eyes and flawless complexion made her the "Belle of the Village". Not only did she have all the necessary qualities but she must have gone to no end of pains to make the best of them.

It was rumoured that she would start to prepare for Evening Service at about 5.30p.m. and the results certainly did her justice. On Sunday nights Gwennie would be seated in the Ladies' Choir, her face exquisitely made up and her golden hair permed into rows and rows of little sausage curls. In the winter the whole lot would be framed by the grey fur collar of her blue coat.

I would be seated behind the pillar, very conscious of my spotty face, straight hair and steel rimmed glasses. How I would envy the glamorous Gwennie and must have been guilty of breaking the tenth commandment over and over again.

Eventually Gwennie married and left the village. Her parents also left the little thatched cottage and one dark winter night it burned to the ground, flames leaping so high from the blazing thatch that they could be seen for miles around.

CHAPTER
TEN

Cricket

The 1930s seemed to have been the heyday for the Heddington and Stockley Cricket Club. Starting as an annual match between the men of Heddington versus those of Stockley, I gather the two teams amalgamated to make one very enthusiastic eleven.

At that time, Dick was appointed Captain, Barbara was the scorer, and Peg and I two of their most enthusiastic supporters. The pitch was situated in the field in front of the cottages, later renamed the "Cricket Field", by which name it is known today, although unfortunately no cricket is played there now.

Then, in those pre-war years, the wicket was carefully prepared by the players, rolled by a large horse roller and mowed by an ancient motor mower. Matches were played with other local village teams and, once or even twice a week during the summer, there would be a home match at Stockley.

The visiting team would arrive by various means. If they lived fairly locally, most of the eleven would arrive on bicycle, with perhaps one car or motor cycle combination bringing the gear. Other times a high old-fashioned bus would drive onto the wide grass verge and disgorge its passengers plus a few of their own supporters.

Folk from Heddington would walk across the fields to watch and give vocal support to their friends. Play would start early on those summer evenings — even so it would be dusk before stumps were drawn.

Peg and I would sit in the shade of the tall elms, by the wooden stile and applaud each and every run by the home side. When they fielded, we mourned each dropped catch but rejoiced when Charlie Hurcombe, the local fast bowler, took wicket after wicket in quick succession.

Looking back, I wonder at the great difference in age of the members of these Village Cricket Teams. There would be a youngster hardly old enough to be at Senior School, whilst at the other end of the scale some veteran, so stiff in limb that he had to have a "runner" while he was batting. This combination rarely worked — the "runner" generally being too enthusiastic, throwing caution to the winds and heading for the opposite crease, in spite of warning shouts from the batsman. This resulted in someone being run out. Uncle Harry, the umpire, would signal the dismissal, remaining completely impassive in spite of occasional barracking from the onlookers stretched out under the hedge. Uncle Harry always wore a straw hat pulled down well against the sun's rays, and his portly form would look even rounder because of the layers of pullovers tied round his middle.

Occasionally a batsman would manage to lift the ball so high in the air that it would clear the high hedge and the green and land on the road. These sixes were rare, but on one hot July evening Audley Chivers hooked one into Reg Marvin's little front garden, narrowly missing the sitting room window. This mammoth shot received a standing ovation from the spectators but scared the life out of Reg's aged mother who was sitting in the front room at the time.

Unnoticed some of our cows would detach themselves from the rest of the herd and leave the field behind the Orchard, grazing their way gradually until they joined the fielders amongst the buttercups in the outfield. Then the game would be halted until they were driven back out of harm's way.

When homework allowed Peg and I accompanied the team for away matches. We were there at Spye Park when a thunderstorm prematurely ended the match. Thunder rolled around the hills and the lightning flashed amongst the trees, illuminating the pitch and the players. Eventually the rain came and we made for the bus before the main torrent descended.

On a glorious Saturday afternoon we watched Heddington and Stockley thrash Bowden Hill. Cars stopped on the side of the narrow road which lead down to Lacock over the bridge. Their occupants sat in the sunshine and watched the match. Peg and I sat in the long grass and rejoiced as the wickets fell. Charlie Hurcombe was on form that sunny afternoon!

Seagry Cricket Team seemed to be composed almost entirely of member of the same family. I imagine they were brothers and cousins. Not only did they all bear the same surname but they all looked alike which must have caused no end of problems for Barbara and her score board. To round it off the father of the majority of the team acted as umpire.

A few local cricketing characters come to mind: Tommy Gartside, the burly roadman, who would exchange his brush and shovel for a wicket keeper's gloves and pads. I can see him quite clearly now, crouched behind the stumps. He was a formidable force and rarely did a ball escape him. At batting, he was a slogger, having a wild swipe at every ball that came, irrespective whether it was on or off the wicket. This generally resulted in rather a short innings though, sometimes, given a little luck, he would make a last wicket stand which would turn the tide of the match, resulting in a victory for Heddington and Stockley.

Tom Teague, the Rector, was another "slogger" although I believe he was also a useful slow bowler and could put a wicked spin to the ball. Once he was felled by a fast ball from the opposition and his long form lay motionless on the pitch for what seemed ages. Peg and I were convinced he was dead and were relieved when the anxious crowd melted away and he started to bat once more.

Among the team were two friends of Dick's from school — Jack Tucker and David Chivers, who because of their sports training played a far more orthodox game with consequently better results. They were not nearly as much fun to watch however!

Most other village teams resembled Heddington and Stockley — keeping going with hard work and enthusiasm but always short of funds and resources.

159

Once during an away match Dick hit a ball way out of the field — a lengthy search failed to find the elusive ball. The home side were unable to produce a replacement. I think in the end one was borrowed from a neighbouring village.

By no means every member of our team, and that would apply to every other village eleven, would sport the conventional whites. There would be a sprinkling of corduroy and grey flannels and several cloth caps amongst the players. Heddington and Stockley did once play a team of bank clerks from Calne — they were all attired in sparkling whites. At least that is how they started the evening but they had reckoned without the cowpats and left looking far from immaculate.

CHAPTER
ELEVEN

Ghosts and Superstitions

Heddington Manor was said to be haunted, a supposition we found most intriguing. The ghost took the form of a tiny woman in a long old-fashioned grey dress. She was supposed to sit, motionless, besides one of the bedroom fireplaces. Plenty of villages had relatives, long since dead, who had apparently witnessed this apparition, but we could not get a first hand account from anyone.

It was only recently when I read Ralph Whitlock's book "*The Folklore of Wiltshire*" that I realised that Stockley too was credited with its own ghost or rather several of them! Years ago, a man stood at the roadside cap in hand, to wait for an approaching funeral procession to pass. Just before it reached him, it vanished. There were no other details as to the exact whereabouts or the actual time of day. I felt quite cheated that we hadn't known all this interesting information when we were children. Perhaps it was just as well, we should no doubt have elaborated on it! A possible explanation could be that the onlooker had imbibed too well at the Ivy Inn!

Whetham House was also believed to be haunted by a Russian gentleman, dressed in a tall hat and a cloak — a man who had been killed in a duel years ago. This ghost was reported to be witnessed by an evacuee during the Second World War who had awakened to find the tall figure bending over him.

That seems to be the account of the only really local ghosts. Further afield shepherds have witnessed, or so they said, a Roman Legion marching near the Cherhill White Horse. Tan Hill was once the scene of a macabre race. Years ago, on a Sunday morning, when steam engines were a novelty in rural areas, two men had a wager. One bet the other that he could drive his two horses pulling a hearse faster than the steam engine. The hearse overturned killing both the horses and the driver. In the half-light of an autumn dawn, this tragedy is supposed to be re-enacted. Apparently a grisly warning to all that no work should be on the Sabbath!

Roundway Down was deemed to be haunted in Victorian times by a human ghost from one of the barrows. We felt that anything could be possible on those desolate downs. Not a ghost story but one that made us feel slightly uneasy was the following, often told and retold by Tom Chivers of Stockley.

One winter afternoon, the Carter from Church Farm was returning from Devizes to Heddington by way of the downs, his empty wagon drawn by a carthorse. Before he had gone a mile or so, a blizzard blew up, snow fell from the leaden sky, covering the grass tracks with a thick carpet and all the familiar landmarks were obliterated by its white mantle.

By this time all the daylight had faded. The Carter decided that to continue his journey under these conditions would be foolhardy, so he unharnessed the horse and, wrapping himself around in a sack, sheltered in under the cart to await the end of the storm.

An hour later, the loose horse cantered into the yard at Church Farm. The anxious farmer alerted the other farm hands. A search was made and the body of the Carter was found — frozen to death beneath his wagon.

Although this had happened long before we were born and we had no personal knowledge of the Carter or for that matter, any of his family, we felt great sorrow for this tragedy. If only the man had stayed with his horse, we told each other.

Some of the older villagers could predict the weather with uncanny accuracy but with a lifetime of studying the pattern of nature this was understandable. The old shepherd who lived in the lonely house on the downs, was very gifted in this way.

All country folk could be termed superstitious, although a lot of it probably stems from old remedies and sayings. Mother would never have snowdrops in the house as she thought they brought ill luck. Apparently two of her Great-Aunts had died in two consecutive Februarys and in each case there had been a bowl of these beautiful white flowers in the house. As the Aunts were extremely elderly and February one of the hardest months for the aged to survive, it could only be coincidence.

Old country remedies were widely used and found in lots of cases to be much better than their modern counterparts. In the autumn, we collected grey tufts of sheep's wool from the wire fencing on the downs and rubbed our burning chilblains with it during the winter months. Some swore that the only sure way to get rid of these swollen painful lumps was to beat them with prickly holly until they bled. We couldn't face the initial pain of this drastic treatment, however, and stuck to the sheep's wool.

Later "Snowfire" was to come on the market — thick cardboard tubes of a greasy substance, which had to be heated before application. When dried, this covered not only the chilblains, but also our socks, with a layer of green grease.

We flew to the "bluebag" when stung by a drowsy bee and held a boiled onion wrapped in flannel against an aching ear. I was always anxious to see if cobwebs really would stop bleeding. The only ones readily available were the ones that festooned the inside of the Granary roof. Laced with dusty barley meal, they look far too unhygienic to put on a fresh cut.

We were all scared of touching the water in which eggs had been boiled in case we got warts. Mrs Flower Ruddle, from Willowbrook, could charm them away. We had doubts about this, as Flower had a beauty on the side of his nose, which must have been there for years. According to Mrs Ruddle, she could do nothing for him. To effect a cure the patient had to have complete faith in her powers, and Flower had none. Although I am sure I had not as much as dipped a finger in the egg saucepan, I developed a wart on my thumb and would have liked to enlist her help but doubted whether my own faith would be sufficient. In the end, I used the well-tried remedy of a piece of cotton tied tightly round the offending brown blemish and, in its own good time, it dropped off.

Mrs Vines, from Yatesbury, who had occult powers, attended the Church Fête at the Heddington Rectory as the fortune-teller. Dressed in gipsy robes and with her wigwam tent set up at the top of the big drive, she soon had a queue of eager customers. With devastating frankness and amazing accuracy she told their fortunes. It was rumoured that a certain parishioner attended Church far more regularly when Mrs Vines tactlessly commented on the brevity of her lifeline!

CHAPTER
TWELVE

By Chara or Train

The Sunday School Outing took place in August each year. Although we were not members, Mother would buy spare seats on the bus and we would join in with the others. This always seemed slightly unfair to me, all the other kids had attended Sunday School dutifully each week whilst we had only gone to the Monthly Children's Service. No doubt the organisers were quite pleased to sell the remaining tickets however.

One year the outing seemed to arranged for Weston-Super-Mare, the next to Weymouth. They never seemed to go much further afield, which was probably just as well in our case. Peg was a bad traveller and Bournemouth would probably have been just that little bit too far!

Auntie Dora would sometimes come to stay for a few days and join us for the trip. It would probably be the only opportunity we had of seeing the sea that year so it always proved a red-letter day. Of course quite often when we got to Weston, the sea would be so far out that we spent the best part of the day playing around on the muddy sands. Then when it was time to go home, the tide would be coming in fast, the high waves breaking on the beach, nearer and nearer to the deck chairs. A walk along the pier would prove interesting as we would spend a lot of time at the amusements. We would feed pennies into the machines and then stand with eyes glued to the apertures watching "Paris By Night" and "What the Butler Saw". We weighed ourselves and got, as an added bonus, our fortunes on the back of the ticket.

If the tide was in or if we were at Weymouth, we bathed, Mother and Auntie Dora joining us in the water. They would playfully dash up and down in the shallow sea, splashing us as they did so and calling out how warm the water was. They could have fooled Peg and me, standing with chattering teeth waist deep in the sea! In the end someone would dip our head and shoulders under the chilly water and from then on it didn't seem too bad.

I can only remember one really wet outing day. We set off in a fine drizzle which, according to the optimists on the bus, would turn to heat. They were wrong, it didn't and as we got nearer to our destination, the drizzle turned to a sheeting rain. When we drove along the promenade to the car park, we looked out at the empty grey sea and a deserted beach. A few rain soaked donkeys huddled together under the pier and the ice cream booths had their awnings pulled down and were deserted.

We spent the morning touring the shops, sheltering in doorways and dashing from "Woolies" to "Marks" under the shelter of our umbrella. It was during one of these sudden bursts of speed that Barbara accidentally removed some lady's hair net on one of the spines of her umbrella. We thought the lady unjustifiably annoyed over this — one would have thought that she had been scalped! A watery sun came out at teatime and we went down to the beach, but everything was wet and uncomfortable, even the deck chairs, and it was too late to bathe.

By the time the bus left, the sky had cleared completely and it looked as if it would be glorious weather on the morrow. How we envied the guests at the "Sea Wynd", the "Belle Vista" and the "Northcliffe" Guest Houses. They were just starting their evening meals at little tables set in the bow windows facing the sea and had tomorrow and the whole week to enjoy the sea and the sands. We had missed our one and only opportunity.

The journey home from these outings always seemed a short one. Our faces stiff and salty from the sea breezes, we half dozed in the warm bus. Bundles of damp seaweed hung from out of the carrier bags and there would be little rivulets of sand all down the gangway.

As a change from Calne, we would sometimes during the summer or winter holidays visit Chippenham or Devizes.

On market days Devizes was a bustling place with plenty of colour and noise. We liked to go there, although we tried to avoid the cattle market where the frightened baby calves mourned, with pathetic cries, for the mothers they had left behind.

168

The Shambles had a great attraction for us. Its tiered stalls piled high with all sorts of things — meat, fish, fruit, dairy products, clothes, jewellery and crockery. The calls of the stallholders would reverberate in the high domed roof.

There was a bus from Heddington on Thursdays. It would look a real country bus on its homeward journey, when in the gangway there would be boxes of chirping chicken and rush baskets laden with groceries. Before the Market Bus service was started, it was more difficult to get to Devizes. One could, of course, cycle all the way but Dunkirk Hill was a long steep haul up which to push one's bike. The alternative was to ride to Sandy Lane, leave the bikes at the isolated little thatched cottage and catch the Chippenham to Devizes bus at the road junction. Somehow we always seemed to get the time of departure wrong and would hang around for ages for the bus to come along.

The Devizes Market was at its most colourful just before Christmas. We looked forward to going there during the Christmas Holidays. Then there would be piles of brightly berried holly and mistletoe in the Market place. The town would be full of Christmas shoppers and the pavements so crowded that people spilled over into the road. If we went into Strong's Café for a cup of tea and a bun, all the tables would be full and the waitresses, their white frilled caps pulled down well over their foreheads, would dart to and fro with their trays.

Towards dark, lights would go on in the streets and the crowds would thin out. The market traders would

169

pack up their stalls. We invariably spent so much time browsing around the threepenny and sixpenny counters in Woolworth's that we would have to run to catch the bus home.

The journey to Chippenham was not an easy cycle ride either. Whichever way one went there was one of the two Derry Hills up which to push one's bike. It was far easier to go there by train from Calne. We would leave our bikes at the station and catch the "Calne Flyer", by which name the little local train was affectionately known. It was a friendly unhurried journey on that small steam train. Quite often the guard would see some late comer sprinting up Station Road and the engine driver would back into the station to wait for the panting passenger.

There was two halts *en route* — Stanley Bridge and Black Dog, both rarely used, especially the latter. Shortly after leaving Chippenham, the ticket collector would ask if there would be any passenger wishing to stop there and if there was no affirmative reply, the little train would puff past the tiny platform without stopping. One of the ticket collectors instead of shouting his request from the end of the carriage would enquire of each individual in what sounded like a voice hushed with conspiracy.

"Anyone for the Black Dog?" he would say. A stranger to the line might be forgiven for thinking that it was rather a scandalous place and that if they alighted there, they would be faced with brightly lit casinos, strip tease joints etc. In fact all they would find would be a little cinder track leading to an unlit country road!

In the Chippenham music shop we would buy sheet music of popular tunes of the day. With the same enthusiasm that the young of today buy pop records, we would purchase "*The Isle of Capri*", "*Home Town*", "*Red Sails in the Sunset*" etc. These, for weeks afterwards Mother and Peg would play over and over again.

CHAPTER
THIRTEEN

May Day Revels and Country Dancing

The Reverend Tom Teague instituted May Day celebrations when he took over the living at Heddington. Mrs Waller was the Head Mistress at the Village School at the time, and she enthusiastically entered into the arrangements.

The May Queen was elected by a ballot — the pupils of the school voting for each other. Harry Huband's pony trap was requisitioned, its wheels decorated with bluebells, primroses, long sprays of Solomon's seals, bunches of wood anemones and any other spring flowers which the children could collect in that particular year. Even Harry's old horse wore a bouquet attached to its harness. The Queen and her attendants (the two girls who were runners up in the popularity stakes) made a triumphant journey round the village. They sat in state on the long trap seat, followed on foot by the rest of the pupils, the girls in white dresses. They too carried flowers — lilacs, wallflowers and tulips from cottage gardens combined with the wild flowers to make this a very colourful procession.

I believe the first May Queen was Caroline Gingell, whose previous claim to fame was her prowess at the High Jump in the Flower Show Sports. There, her dress tucked into her navy knickers, her long legs would clear the bar at quite alarming heights! On this first May and this inaugural celebration, however, those long legs were covered by her ankle length white dress and she looked dignified and beautiful.

The procession would make its way slowly past the farm, along the narrow road past Willowbrook and the Common. The old horse would slow down for the slight gradient behind. Encouraged by the helping hand, it would break into a trot and the onlookers would run to catch up with the retinue.

When the Church was reached, there was a Service in which we invariably sang "*All things bright and beautiful*", which sounded just right for the occasion.

The actual crowning ceremony took place in the Manor Garden — if the weather was unkind we repaired to the school. There was a tea and entertainment. Songs with a rural flavour were sung but not necessarily ones to do with May Day in particular. I can remember "*The Ash Grove*" and also Brahms' "*Cradle Song*", neither of which seem to have any bearing on the celebrations.

All through Mr Teague's incumbency we had these May Day revels. Each year a new Queen was chosen — the lovely Gwennie, Jean Arrowsmith, Barbara Hughes and several more, all in turn were carried by Harry's horse and trap in triumph round the village. Only once did the celebrations take on a rather sour turn, the year

173

that the chosen Queen, not any of the above I hasten to add, was found to have bribed the younger children to gain the coveted title. Mrs Waller was deeply shocked at the "nobbling".

Mrs Waller was also responsible for arranging several other village activities, one of which was Country Dancing. All available girls were persuaded to take part. The boys were not so forthcoming — in fact she had no male recruits.

Once a week we met in the school and went through our right and left "allemandes". The culmination of all this practise was to be a display on the Manor Lawn in July. The older girls and those good at sewing agreed to make the dresses for the dancers. At that time there was on the market a material called "Miss Muffet Print" which sold for the remarkably low figure of sixpence a yard. Thus for the princely sum of one shilling and sixpence, one had a summer dress.

In view of the absence of male partners Mrs Waller, resourceful as ever, decreed that those girls who undertook the men's steps should have blue print dresses and their partners could have the pink. Barbara was a boy as were most of the taller, older girls, but Peg and I, dressed in pink with ribbons in our hair, partnered our "blue frocked" gents throughout the Virginian Reel!

The day of the performance arrived and it was a fine, dry evening. The piano was pulled out onto the gravel and, in front of the assembled village audience, we went through our repertoire. It was quite a simple matter to dance when one was comparatively near the piano but, as we promenaded across the lawn, the sound of the music drifted away towards Kings Play and the downs and it was difficult to keep in tune with the others.

To augment the sound of the piano, Mrs Waller would hum. When it became obvious that we had lost the rhythm, she would stand on tiptoe and hum louder and louder, her little round face becoming pinker and pinker until it seemed that she would either explode or take off like a gas filled balloon. When we got our steps to match up with the music once more, she would relax and the humming would cease.

CHAPTER
FOURTEEN

Whist, Drama & Dancing

The wooden Legion Hut was normally the venue for Village Whist Drives. After some practise at home and a solemn undertaking from both of us that we would not, under any circumstances, refer to clubs as clovers, Peg and I were allowed to attend.

Pete Smith was MC and he really put his heart and soul into this task.

"Hearts, Hearts are trumps." he would call, blow his whistle and dart from table to table, shepherding the winning couples in the right direction. Then he might be called upon to settle arguments and to sign the cards of those fortunate enough to score ten or over. The whole procedure would then start all over again, in fact he was never still for any length of time.

The stove in the hut would be stoked up, fresh coal shovelled into the top so that sparks flew out of the bottom. The room would get so hot that it would be a relief when a late comer would let in a blast of cold air as they entered, making the oil lamps swing backwards and forwards on their chains attached to the wooden roof. The whole set up was such a fire hazard that it would make a modern day Fire Officer blanch! The stove was not always so accommodating — with the wind in the wrong direction, smoke would billow from the firebox in the bottom. Then windows would be opened to let out the acrid black cloud and we would sit with streaming eyes in the draughty atmosphere.

Peg soon established herself as quite a competent whist player. She even won prizes, once a joint of beef, a useful addition to the larder! I seemed to lack the concentration necessary and my thoughts would wander at the wrong times. I would glance around the walls at the Union Jack above the photograph of the Reverend Clifton, the little bunch of poppies left over from the Armistice Service and I would start thinking about the Great War, only to realise with something akin to panic that I had no idea what were trumps! Short of actually revoking, I probably made every other possible wrong moves. Ignoring all my partner's hints to lead with a certain suit, I would blandly go my own way; even the inaudible mutters and sighs of my unfortunate partners failed to get through to me. In the warm room I would drowsily try to gather my thoughts together and concentrate on the game but it was hopeless.

Concerts were sometimes held in the Hut. A portable stage was set up in front of the little annexe, which we used as a dressing room. Because this made the dressing room floor much lower than the stage, the cast had to remember to bend their heads low and step high when they went "on stage". This made them look rather like circus horses. If they entered upright they received such a blow on the head from the door lintel that their first few lines were uttered in a bemused state!

A stormy night for the show could bring its problems. A light storm of rain pattering on the corrugated iron roof was distracting but a deluge sounded like machine gun fire and the audience in the back seats failed to hear anything from the stage.

When the Legion Hut proved too small for a village event, the school was called into use. With the partition, which normally divided the two main classrooms were taken down, there was quite a lot of space. Mr Waller produced several plays in the school. There was more dressing room space there than we had enjoyed in the Hut, although we still had to make do with a stage built in sections. At the end of one performance, whilst the entire cast lined up for "The King", one of the back sections of the stage collapsed. Several of the artists disappeared from view, which must have made it very puzzling for the audience.

Mr Waller ambitiously produced "*Eldorado*" and "*The Dear Departed*", which were very enthusiastically received in spite of several prompts. He also wrote and produced "*The Lottery Ticket*" — a comedy with Dick as the leading man. As far as I know that was the last time he ever "trod the boards"!

We had to wait until we left school before we had the chance to take a major part in the concerts. The Wallers had left the village by this time and Barbara produced one or two of the later concerts. Peg was very useful as

178

the pianist but wasn't too enthusiastic about taking part in the sketches. She put it down to the fact that she had an unfortunate stage debut. The first part she undertook entailed her climbing onto the stage from the front. This entrance she had to repeat several times and every time there would be a prolonged clapping from Mr A. I. Hillier who was seated in the front row. Interspersed with the clapping there would be an occasional "Well done, Peggy", "Bravo!" or "Encore! Encore!". It was all meant to be encouraging but Peg found it rather embarrassing to be singled out for excessive applause when she had such a small part.

One winter we were asked to repeat our show at Calstone. We cycled there one dark draughty January evening. Their Village Reading Room had far less facilities than Heddington School did. Originally intended for "Penny Readings" in Victorian times, it did not boast a stage and, as far as I can remember, we performed in a space in the middle of the room. The audience sat around us in a circle, those at the back standing up and leaning against the walls so that they could get an uninterrupted view of the entertainment.

There were screens and wooden clotheshorses, draped with curtains, which screened us from this audience. When we were ready to start, at a given signal, the curtains were whisked away and the cast and the set were revealed. It also revealed the prompter seated self-consciously at the side with her book!

We specialised in the Mable Constanduros type of comedy sketches. Comedy we found most popular, in fact it was a waste of time attempting anything else.

During the war years, Barbara tired a little of Grandma Buggins and her impossible family, and thought that a straight drama would be a change for both the actors and the audience. We therefore rehearsed a most dramatic sketch with Barbara taking the main female part. The climax of the play and her moment of glory was the part where she was strangled whilst sitting on a park bench. The role of the strangler was taken by one of the bell ringers and the park bench was a borrowed garden seat. On the night everything went wrong, the audience failed to treat Barbara's big scene with the "hushed silence" it deserved. One could hardly blame them, they had always found plenty to chortle at during previous Heddington shows and they couldn't see why this one should be different. They roared with laughter during Barbara's anguished cries for help and when she realistically dropped lifelessly to the ground, the applause was deafening.

The partition in the school would also be taken down for Village Dances. For the sum of one shilling and sixpence, which included lemonade and biscuits, we did our best to valetta, fox-trot and waltz, accompanied by a volunteer on the school piano.

Devoid of make up, small talk and still very much schoolchildren, Peg and I were not very sought after as partners. "Paul Jones" were our salvation, when with a bit of luck, we might find a partner who was duty bound to put up with us for two or three minutes.

In my youthful opinion, the Gingell brothers were the very epitome of rhythmic elegance and I longed to be as graceful as Henry in the waltz! It was indeed a fortunate moment for me when the music stopped when I was opposite him. He told me once, when I was quick stepping all over his feet as the pianist played a slow foxtrot, that he had learned to dance by practising with a chair to gramophone records. Seized with the desire to do likewise I practised round and round the bathroom clutching one of our cane bottomed bedroom chairs humming tunes in what I fondly imagined to be three-four time. However it was years later and when I had lost a considerable amount of "puppy-fat" that I really managed to get both feet to do what I wanted — together and at the right time.

CHAPTER
FIFTEEN

Growing Up

We entered the Fifth form and were within two years of the School Certificate and leaving school. Peg decided that she would come home to work on the farm and, partly because I had no particular leaning that direction, and partly because two of us wouldn't be needed in any case, I decided that I'd find something else to do. Just precisely what that would be was in the laps of the gods, jobs being desperately hard to find in the late 1930s.

Peg therefore joined the Young Farmers' Club and, like the rest of the members, started to rear a calf for the local competition. I was not encouraged to join, I suppose the chances of "calf rearing" being of any practical use in my future career were too remote. Looking back I suppose that would be the first time we were encouraged to have individual interests.

Peg's first calf was Strawberry, a pretty roan coloured animal with a white face. Peg lavished much time and a lot of affection on Strawberry, with the result that she became fonder of the human race than she did of her own species. The day of the judging arrived, Peg anxious that Strawberry should not go to "fresh fields and pastures new", persuaded Dad to attend the auction that followed the judging and buy Strawberry back, so that she could eventually join our own milking herd at the farm. Peg, in her white coat and "wellies", anxiously watched from the side as Strawberry was led into the ring in front of the auctioneer and bidding commenced. There must have been rather too long a pause when the bidding was against Dad as, much to the amusement of the crowd, an anxious voice called out "Bid up, Dad!"

All was well and Strawberry came back home. This proved to be rather a mixed blessing, as she remained as playful as ever and as fond of the human race. On seeing anybody in the field when she was grazing, she would leave the rest of the cows and frolic up. What would have been a playful "bunt" in the rear from a tiny calf now became a painful charge from a large horned headed cow. All Peg's hand reared calves turned out the same, even old age and motherhood didn't subdue their enthusiasm.

Peg called Strawberry's successors after the teachers at school. There was Hilda, a handsome black and white Friesian, called after Miss Stephens the headmistress, and Alex, a young steer, after Alexander Purvis, our handsome Geography Master. Amazing as it may sound, the teachers seemed quite pleased to think that they had bovine namesakes.

My one venture into farming was to rear some cockerels in a little fowl house, with a run, in the vegetable garden near the orchard hedge. I don't quite know what started me on this, probably the idea that it would be a profitable exercise. The day-old chicks were certainly reasonable at one penny each. I bought twelve from Devizes Market, plus a cashbook from Smith's in which to do the costing. I bought meal and corn from Mother, weighing it out pound by pound laboriously on the old scales in the Granary. The cockerels grew from little pale fluffy chicks to leggy half-grown birds in a very short while. It was then that they started to consume great troughs of mash daily and, as I glumly totted up my "food bills", the idea that I was a budding tycoon receded somewhat! In the end my resources being nil, I was forced to barter some of my stock in exchange for food for the rest of the hungry birds. The net profit was so minute that it put me off keeping poultry for years!

As we grew older, we did more work on the farm during weekends and in the evenings. The two main tasks in the spring seemed to be "muck spreading" and stone picking. "Muck spreading" wasn't the disagreeable job it sounded. All through the early part of the year, Bonnie, Trooper or Violet had pulled the loaded dung cart from the yards to the fields and Dad or one of the men had thrown the manure out into neat heaps and in regular rows all over the fields. Our job was to spread it evenly all over the grass and, by the time we had to handle it, it was neither odorous nor unpleasant. It was quite time consuming and it didn't pay to hurry. If one loaded the fork with too much, at the end of half an hour one felt as if one's arms were being pulled from their sockets.

Later on in the spring, Peg and I would walk all over the same fields, heads bent, looking for all the stray stones which could have been scraped off the cobbled yards and found their way out into the fields with the manure. It could be quite a pleasant task if it was a warm spring day with the April sun beating down on our backs and the cuckoo calling from the hedgerows. However, far too often, there would be a chill wind blowing and our fingers would get frozen as they came in contact with the cold stones. Then the chilly whiteness of the blackthorn blossom would gleam in the hedges and the primroses would appear to shrink back behind their thick leaves. Here again this was not a job to be hurried, a large stone left undetected beneath a big tuft of grass could, later on, break the knives of a mowing machines.

In the summer there was haymaking, which could be a lengthy business in a wet season. Peg and I generally helped either on the rick or on the load at the foot of the elevator. Being on the rick could be rather nerve racking, especially during the last few loads, when the sides got really steep. It could mean sliding down a few feet to find the head of the ladder, which would be half buried in the long loose hay. "Throwing off" was perhaps easier, there didn't seem quite the urgency and the "throwers off" more of less dictated the pace of the work. I can't say that I liked haymaking. One was always busy when the weather was good, in which case there would be far more exciting things to do. Unlike other jobs on the farm, there always seemed a desperate urgency about it, always more fields to cut when one was finished and always the chance, even in a fine hot spell that it might "brew up for thunder". On the rick or on the load, it was a hot, sweaty job, perspiration would stream down our necks and bare legs and the hayseeds would stick on our wet skin making it itch intolerably.

Occasionally there would be more pleasant tasks in the fields, such as raking out the back swathe, but even then one felt guilty if one didn't work full out. There was always this compulsion to get things done before the weather broke.

Autumn, always my favourite season of the year, meant apple picking and storing, but that could prove a pleasant unhurried job. One could take one's time sorting all the fruit and putting everything that was absolutely sound on the wide shelves in the box room. The fallers, the bruised and the blemished would be put aside to be used first of all. Some years would be one of those golden autumn days when the sun shone from a cloudless sky and when only the shortness of the days made one realise that the year was getting old.

Throughout every season there were always the hens, demanding attention daily — "letting out", feeding twice a day and then "shutting up" at night. In the summer all this had to be fitted in with other jobs. In the winter they could be even more of a nuisance, especially in frosty weather when their drinking water froze immediately it was poured into their drinking vessels and locks froze on the hen house doors and had to be thawed out with hot water.

186

The hen houses had to be creosoted at regular intervals, but I rather enjoyed painting the dark "tar smelling" liquid all over the shabby boards. One had to use a moderate amount of care as creosote could stain clothes and burn one's skin if used recklessly. However there was something rather rewarding when the chore was done and the house stood clean, sterilised and with all the faded sun scorched wood now a deep dark oak shade.

CHAPTER
SIXTEEN

Church and Chapel

On Wednesday nights during one cold wet Lenten time, the Reverend Teague held lantern lectures in the Church. His "Magic Lantern", as we called it, would have been termed an antique even in the 1930s and one was never quite sure what should be shown next on the wide sheet hung above the Chancel steps.

The slides had a way of being projected sideways on, upside down, and crooked. Sometimes they missed the makeshift screen altogether and appeared on the pulpit — the colours muted and the figures misshapen against the carved oak.

Once a dramatic slide depicting Angels arising from tombs and flying heavenwards towards a bright blue sky and fluffy white clouds was shown upside down. Thus the Angels appears to be diving headfirst into a frothy blue ocean! This puzzled the audience and convulsed the organ blower.

I can vaguely remember other talks in the church, most very dim memories but one is still a vivid recollection. Given by a man who had spent most of his life helping in a Leper Colony. It made quite an impression on my youthful mind. I guess this tale rightly belongs to the first part of my book — I must have been very young at the time. The morning following the talk I became firmly convinced that somehow or other I had contracted that deadly disease.

"I'm sure I'm a leper!" I confided to Peg, showing her a small white mark in the palm of my hand. Peg agreed that she thought that without a doubt I was right and with great presence of mind prepared the following plan. In Jack Daw there was a derelict fowl house, formerly used to house broody hens. It had stood empty for some time. With two wheels missing, it sprawled under the overhanging boughs of a willow tree — one side completely hidden by stinging nettles, tarred felt flapping from the roof and its door swinging backwards and forwards from rusty hinges. There I was to stay and Peg would bring me food three times a day leaving it outside the trap door. I was to watch through the dusty chicken wire covering the window until she had crossed the footbridge over the brook before I opened the door to get the food. On no account was I to come out before or the family and perhaps the entire village would be in danger.

Together we inspected the makeshift Isolation Hospital. Although it had not held poultry for some time, I felt that red mites were probably still lurking at the end of the dilapidated perches and in the corners of the nest boxes. Perhaps because of being eaten alive with red mite seemed a fate nearly as bad as leprosy, I went and told Mother all about it. She immediately scotched the leprosy theory saying "That I was a caution to be sure". According to parents and relatives one was either a "caution" or a "Cough Drop" if one did or said anything unconventional.

I told Peg the good news. It may have been my imagination but she seemed disappointed that all her carefully laid plans were not to be put into operation.

Heddington Non-Conformist Chapel, a little red brick building, was midway between the Church and Common. I should think that I had probably reached the Fourth form at School when I undertook a sort of thesis on "Rural Religion". Everyone in the form was doing some sort of project as a holiday task. Having written quite a lot about St Andrew's, Heddington, I turned my attention to other denominations.

Regular services were held in the Chapel. They were arranged by the Miss Browns, two maiden ladies from Splatts, who must have been its mainstay and probably two of its most regular worshippers. Mrs Hughes played the organ which stood on the dais along with the reading desk.

Taking advantage of the fact that it was the Chapel Centenary and therefore quite an important landmark in its history, I decided to attend the service to commemorate it. Armed with a notebook and pencil, I sat in one of the back seats, making copious notes during the hymns and the address. Peg didn't accompany me, I can only think she must have been doing a project on something else, or perhaps she thought that it seemed rather like gate-crashing to attend another Denominational Service.

The service over, we had cups of tea and seed cake and I was included and handed some eats. Even then I was still scribbling my impressions. If the rest of the Congregation were puzzled why I, from a staunch Anglican family, was seated in one of their back pews, they did not show it. In fact I was cordially shaken by the hand after the service and they waved me off as I pedalled away on my bike, the pages of my notebook full of important data.

TAILPIECE

Our last summer at school meant a lot of hard work studying for the Oxford School Certificate. I think that this must have absolved us from taking too big a part in the haymaking for that particular year.

The summer was, I recollect, hot and dry for most of the time. During the warm summer evenings, Peg and I spent hours revising schoolwork in the open air. One Saturday afternoon both of us were sitting on the headland in More Mead as the freshly mown grass dried in the sun. The row of elms in the opposite hedge seemed to waver in the heat from the burning sky. We read through Byron's poems and then started to test each other with contexts from the set Shakespearean Play. It was probably forty years later when I saw "*Romeo and Juliet*" dramatised on television. It brought back quite vividly the scent of dog roses and hay from a midsummer years go when we were trying to apportion correctly each speech between Capulets and Montagues.

The last Assembly before the school holidays could be quite a moving occasion even if one would be returning to school at the beginning of the following term. However when it meant leaving for good, it would be most nostalgic and emotional.

"*God dismiss us with Thy Blessing*" we sang with lumps in our throats on that morning in late July. Peg was going home to her life of chicken rearing on the farm and I was to haunt the Labour Exchange for a few weeks until I found a job.

If we were worried by the recent start of the Civil War in Spain or the obvious unrest in Europe, we were reassured by one look at our school atlas where so much of the World's areas was still coloured pink. We had immense faith in our own country as a World power. Nearer home Edward VIII had been proclaimed King since January and we were more intrigued than worried about the Mrs Simpson problem.

For the first time our lives divided somewhat. We would have our own friends and lead a more separate existence. I should not preface most of my remarks with "Peg and I" but, for the rest of my life, I would be grateful for all the shared experiences of a very happy childhood.

Potato

ISIS publish a wide range of books in large print, from fiction to biography. Any suggestions for books you would like to see in large print or audio are always welcome. Please send to the Editorial department at:

ISIS Publishing Ltd.
7 Centremead
Osney Mead
Oxford OX2 0ES
(01865) 250 333

A full list of titles is available free of charge from:
Ulverscroft large print books

(UK)
The Green
Bradgate Road, Anstey
Leicester LE7 7FU
Tel: (0116) 236 4325

(Australia)
P.O Box 953
Crows Nest
NSW 1585
Tel: (02) 9436 2622

(USA)
1881 Ridge Road
P.O Box 1230, West Seneca,
N.Y. 14224-1230
Tel: (716) 674 4270

(Canada)
P.O Box 80038
Burlington
Ontario L7L 6B1
Tel: (905) 637 8734

(New Zealand)
P.O Box 456
Feilding
Tel: (06) 323 6828

Details of **ISIS** complete and unabridged audio books are also available from these offices. Alternatively, contact your local library for details of their collection of **ISIS** large print and unabridged audio books.

Rolato